SOUTH DEVON & DARTMOOR

Teashop Walks

Jean Patefield

COUNTRYSIDE BOOKS
NEWBURY BERKSHIRE

First published 1997
© Jean Patefield 1997

COUNTRYSIDE BOOKS
3 Catherine Road
Newbury Berkshire

ISBN 1 85306 462 9

To Bill Patefield,
a very dear father-in-law

Designed by Graham Whiteman
Cover illustration by Colin Doggett
Photographs and maps by the author

Produced through MRM Associates Ltd., Reading
Printed by Woolnough Bookbinding Ltd., Irthlingborough

Contents

Introduction

Walk

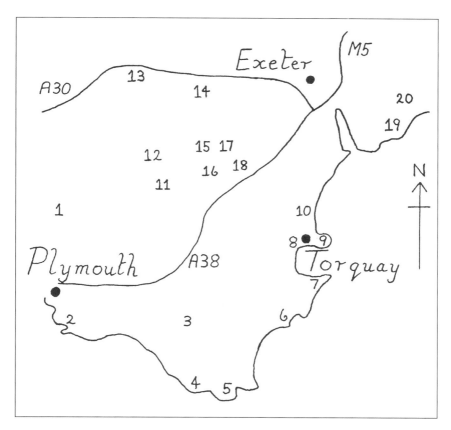

Area map showing the locations of the walks.

KEY TO SKETCH MAPS

Path on route	– – →	Sea	~ ~ ~	Point in text	⑥
Path not on route	...	Church	†	Car park	▢
Road	═══	Teashop	☕	Building referred to in text	▪
River	〜〜〜	Pub refered to in text	PH	Quarry (disused)	⟳
		Summit	▲		

Introduction

Devon is one of England's largest counties. It has two coastlines, two cities, one complete national park and part of another. This book contains 20 walks which explore the south of the county. This includes Dartmoor National Park, the attractive rolling countryside south of the moor and east of Exeter, and Devon's south coast. The walks have been chosen to visit each type of scenery. Some explore the wild uplands of Dartmoor, others visit the dramatic valleys round its edge. Several walks make use of the South West Coast Path and some explore the rich farmland between. It is difficult to think of anywhere else in England where such variety could be enjoyed in such a relatively small area.

The walks in this book are all between 2½ and 6 miles and should be within the capacity of the average person, including those of mature years and families with children. They are intended to take the walker through some of the loveliest scenery in England at a gentle pace with plenty of time to stop and stare, to savour the beauty and interest all around. A dedicated yomper and stomper could probably knock off the whole book in a single weekend but in doing so they would have missed the point and seen nothing. To fully appreciate the countryside it is necessary to go slowly with your eyes and ears open.

The different types of scenery have their origins in the different rocks beneath the surface and in the way the land has been used in 8,000 years of human occupation. Certain activities have disappeared: we no longer think of Devon as a tin mining area, for example. Some of Devon's sons and daughters have been important and famous people; others are just as interesting but more obscure. Such a long history has left its mark on the countryside and buildings so there is much that is fascinating to see and this can add enormously to the pleasure of a walk. In addition, there is a wealth of wildlife interest. Therefore, as well as giving directions for the route itself, I have also included information about the interesting geology, history and wildlife to be seen on the way.

Some of the walks involve a little climbing, inevitable as hills and cliffs add enormous interest to the countryside and much of Devon is so attractive because it is so rolling. However, this presents no problem to the sensible walker who has three uphill gears - slowly, very slowly and admiring the view. None of the walks in this book are inherently hazardous but sensible care should be taken. A lot of the falls that do happen are due to unsuitable footwear, particularly smooth soles since steep grass can be as slippery as the more obviously wet rock. Proper walking shoes or boots also give some protection to the ankle. It is, of course, essential to watch where you place your feet to avoid tripping. Wainwright, the doyen of walkers in the Lake District, said that he never had a serious fall in all his years and thousands of miles of walking because he always looked where he put his feet and stopped if he wanted to admire the scenery.

All the routes are on public rights of way or permissive paths and have been carefully checked, but things do change in the countryside; a gate is replaced by a stile or a wood is extended. Each walk is circular and is illustrated by a sketch map. An Ordnance Survey sheet is useful as well, especially for identifying the main features of views. There are several from which to choose. The area is covered by the Landranger 1:50 000 ($1\frac{1}{4}$ inches to 1 mile) series, sheets 191, 192, 201 and 202. Dartmoor is covered on one 1:25 000 ($2\frac{1}{2}$ inches to 1 mile) map in the Outdoor Leisure series and South Devon on another. The rest is covered by the standard Pathfinder 1:25 000 maps. The grid reference of the starting point and the appropriate Landranger map are given for each walk.

The walks are designed so that, starting where suggested, the teashop is reached in the second half so a really good appetite for tea can be worked up and then its effects walked off. Some walks begin at a car park, which is ideal. Where this is not possible, the suggested starting place will always have somewhere where a few cars can be left without endangering other traffic or causing inconvenience. However, it sometimes fits in better with the plans for the day to start and finish at the teashop and for each walk there are details of how to do this.

Tea is often said to be the best meal to eat out in England and this is doubly true in Devon, home of that famous delicacy - clotted cream! It is the richest, most fattening and wickedly delicious ambrosia. The best clotted cream is made from the milk of Jersey cows which have grazed Devon's lush pasture. This is heated gently for a long period of time so the cream forms a crust on top which is skimmed off.

I believe tea is a meal to be enjoyed on all possible occasions but if it is something you can experience only rarely then surely Devon is the place to do so. Scones with cream and strawberry jam, delicious home-made cakes, toasted teacakes dripping with butter in winter, delicate cucumber sandwiches in summer, all washed down with the cup that cheers! Bad for the figure maybe, but the walking will see to that.

The best teashops offer a range of cakes, all home-made and including fruit cake as well as scones and other temptations. Cream teas should, of course, feature clotted cream. Teapots should be capacious and pour properly. Ideally, there should be an attractive garden where tea can be taken outside in summer. Most of the teashops visited on these walks fulfil all these criteria admirably - and they all serve a good tea.

Teashops are not scattered evenly throughout South Devon and Dartmoor. In some places popular with tourists, the visitor is spoilt for choice. In such cases the teashop which, in the author's opinion, most closely fulfils the criteria set out above is recommended but, should that not appeal, there are others from which to choose. In other places where there is a delightful walk to be enjoyed the choice for tea may be more limited so a few of the teashops visited on the circuits in this book are in unusual places such as gardens and stately homes. However, that in itself adds interest to the walk and they all offer a good tea partway round an attractive walk.

The opening times and telephone number of each teashop are given. Many are rather vague about when they open out of season: it seems to depend on weather and mood. If you are planning a walk on a wet November Tuesday, for example, a call to check that tea will actually be available that day is a wise precaution. Some are definitely closed in the winter and for these walks an alternative source of refreshment is given where ever possible. In most cases, these are pubs serving food which in some instances includes tea.

So put on your walking shoes and prepare to be delighted, by the lovely Devon countryside and a traditional Devon tea!

Jean Patefield

Walk 1
BUCKLAND ABBEY

This interesting walk, just outside the boundary of Dartmoor National Park, uses quiet field paths and lanes to link two attractive villages and Buckland Abbey. The highlight of the route is undoubtedly Buckland Abbey which is owned by the National Trust and houses the teashop for today's walk (entry charge for non-members). It has a long and fascinating history from 13th-century monastery to country house and this is very well illustrated by the displays. Particularly engrossing are those about the life of its most famous resident, Sir Francis Drake.

 At Buckland Abbey the National Trust teashop is situated in the building which was once the abbot's guest house. It serves cream teas and delicious cakes as well as an extensive range of ice creams. It is open from 10.30 am until 5.30 pm between 1st April and the end of October. In the winter, from November to March, it is open on Saturday and Sunday afternoons. The extensive courtyard is surrounded by craft workshops and you can watch the craftsmen at work. In addition, there is an audio-visual presentation about the Abbey's history. Telephone: 01822 855024.

When the teashop is closed, an alternative source of refreshment on this walk is the Who'd Have Thought It!, the pub in Milton Combe, which serves an excellent selection of bar food.

DISTANCE: 4 miles.

MAP: OS Landranger 201 Plymouth and Launceston.

HOW TO GET THERE: From the A386 Tavistock to Plymouth road, follow the signs to Buckland Monachorum from Horrabridge. There is a car park on the left which belongs to the church and may be used by visitors except near the times of services.

STARTING POINT: Buckland Monachorum church car park (GR 490682).

ALTERNATIVE STARTING POINT: If you want to visit the teashop at the beginning or end of your walk, start at Buckland Abbey where there is ample parking in the National Trust car park. The teashop is inside the Abbey buildings. You will then start the walk at point 9.

THE WALK

Buckland Monachorum is an appealing village with a pleasing mixture of buildings. The present church is mainly 15th century but is on the site of a much older building, there having been a church here since Celtic times. Inside is a list of incumbents. Some of them have served this parish for a very long time - three of them over 60 years. The most remarkable must be Joseph Rowe who was vicar from 1646 to 1708. These were times of great religious and political upheaval covering the later years of the Civil War, the Commonwealth and Restoration through to the reign of Queen Anne. He must have been very adept at going with the flow and keeping his head down!

1. From the car park turn left through the village. At the church turn right on a public footpath by the churchyard. Over a stone stile turn right. After a bridge continue ahead along the right-hand side of two fields to a lane.

2. Turn left for 100 yards and then take a public footpath on the right up some steps. Follow the path along the right-hand side of a field to a stile in a dip. In the next field the path is not apparent on the ground: bear half-left to a stile.

3. The stile gives onto a track at a fork. Take the branch ahead and follow it to a lane.

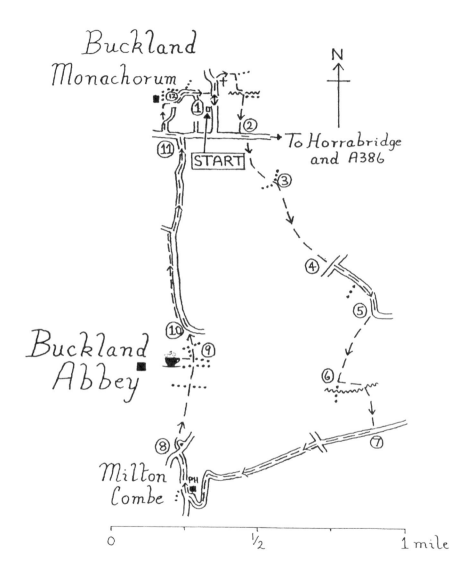

Buckland
Monachorum

To Horrabridge
and A386

START

Buckland
Abbey

Milton
Combe

N

0   ½   1 mile

4. Take the lane directly opposite for about ¼ mile.

5. As the lane bends left, take a public footpath on the right and head half-right to a gate in the middle of the hedge at the far end of the field. Continue in the same direction down the left-hand side of the next field to another gate.

6. Immediately through the gate turn left. Walk along the left-hand side of a field, dipping down to cross a stream and then up to a small gate. Continue in the same direction along the left-hand side of a field to a gate onto a lane.

7. Turn right. Continue straight ahead at some crossroads. Follow this lane down into the village of Milton Combe, past the pub and uphill to a road junction.

Milton Combe is a very attractive village, nestling in the valley. The pub, which you walk past (or not!), is the Who'd Have Thought It! The village's pub used to be in the building which now houses the post office and it was called the First and Last. The person who owned the building which houses the present pub applied for a licence. It took so long to come that he had rather lost hope. When it arrived he shouted 'Who'd have thought it!' and so the pub got its name. The picture over the porch shows this scene with the disgruntled owner of the old pub in the background.

☕ **8.** At the top of the hill go straight across the road and take a public footpath opposite. This passes by a bus turning circle to a stile and then along the left-hand side of a field. Cross a track and go through a wooden kissing-gate opposite. Continue in the same direction over the next field, across a drive and ahead on a track to a second drive. Turn left to the entrance to Buckland Abbey.

Buckland Abbey was a Cistercian house founded by monks from the Isle of Wight in 1278. After the Dissolution it was sold to Sir Richard Grenville for £233 3s 4d. Its first occupant as a private house was his son Roger who went down with the Mary Rose. Roger's son Richard did most of the conversion to a private house. This project was helped with money he had made with the privateer Castle of Comfort. He then sold it to Francis Drake who had made a fortune from his pioneering voyage round the world. The displays and memorabilia are fascinating. They include the famous Drake's Drum, supposed to sound whenever England is in peril. Drake's exploits have made him a heroic, almost mythical, figure, rather like King Arthur. The excellently presented displays show him to be a man of his times, not above a bit of what today would be considered sharp practice. Drake died of dysentery on the

Spanish Main in 1596, leaving no children. The line was continued by his brother and the last of the Drake family to own Buckland Abbey sold the property in 1943, when it was given to the National Trust.

9. After visiting Buckland Abbey and tea, return to the point where you joined the entrance drive and turn left through a metal kissing-gate to continue on the path you were on before. Bear slightly right to a gate and then follow the path across yet another drive to emerge on a lane.

10. Turn left, using the path on the left side of the road for part of the way. Pass the junction with the road to Bere Alston on the left and carry on to a T-junction.

11. Turn left and then right at Cuxton Meadows. After 25 yards, when the road bends right, continue in the same direction on a track. Just before a farm turn right.

12. At the end of the path turn left and then right. When the road bends right continue on a path between houses, back to the centre of Buckland Monachorum.

Walk 2
WEMBURY

This is a short walk with wonderful views of the Yealm estuary and inland. The highlight is a stretch of coast path which leads down to Wembury Marine Conservation Area, noted for its superb shore life. Wembury Marine Centre (Telephone: 01752 862538) gives visitors an introduction to the animals and plants of the coast and sea and there are guided rock pool rambles in the summer. Of course, if you want to explore this fascinating wildlife, it is important to time your arrival about low water. After tea at Wembury Mill, the return is a short walk along the side of a valley.

The Old Mill is an old mill house more or less on the beach and it is owned by the National Trust. It houses a shop and a café which serves mugs and cups of tea with cream teas and cakes. There is also a delicious range of ice creams. An attractive area outside makes good use of the old millstones. It is open between 10.30 am and 5 pm from 1st April to the end of October and sometimes at the weekend in November and December. Telephone: 01752 862314.

When the teashop is closed, the only alternative source of refreshment on this walk is the Odd Wheel, which is near the start (or the finish).

DISTANCE: $3\frac{1}{2}$ miles.

MAP: OS Landranger 201 Plymouth and Launceston.

HOW TO GET THERE: From the A379 Plymouth to Kingsbridge road, follow the signs to Wembury from Elburton, 4 miles east of Plymouth. The directions start from Wembury Primary School. This is on the left on the way into Wembury, just after a shop on the right and just before a pub, the Odd Wheel, on the right. There are several spots nearby where a car can be left without causing inconvenience to local residents.

STARTING POINT: Wembury Primary School, West Wembury (GR 496528).

ALTERNATIVE STARTING POINT: If you want to visit the teashop at the beginning or end of your walk, start at Wembury Beach where there is ample parking in the National Trust car park. The teashop is by the car park. You will then start the walk at point 6.

THE WALK

1. Facing the school, turn left. Opposite the shops take a public footpath on the right, signed 'Brownhill Lane'. At the end of the gardens turn left and after 40 yards turn right up some steps and across a field.

2. At the end of the field carry on in the same direction on a path initially between a fence and a wall and then along the left-hand side of the field. Ignore a path on the right.

3. At a lane, turn right along the lane.

4. When the lane makes a sharp right-hand bend, by a barn, continue ahead on a public footpath signed 'ferry and coastal path'.

The views along this stretch of coast, owned by the National Trust, are stunning. The large rock (or small island) seen offshore is the Great Mew Stone which has been inhabited at various times. In 1744 a local man was banished to it for seven years and took his family with him. His daughter, known as Black Joan, stayed on with her husband and three children when her father's exile was over and only left when her husband was drowned rowing to the island. In the early 1800s one Samuel Wakeman and his wife Ann lived there with an eye to the early tourist trade. He produced publicity material about the island, cut steps to make exploring the island

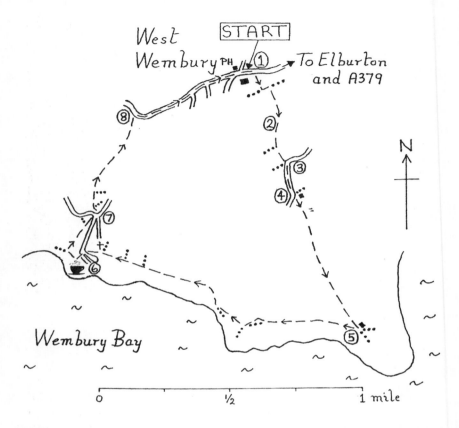

easier, especially for the ladies, and rowed visitors across. This entrepreneurial character had to leave when he was caught smuggling.

☕ **5.** Turn right immediately after a small cottage called Rocket House. Continue on this path, first by the Yealm estuary and then along the cliffs, to the teashop.

Like so many other parts of the Devon coast, this area has a history of shipwrecks. For example, the John *ran aground on the Blackstone Rocks below the cliffs in 1824. James Cragg, a Yealm boatman, was posted guard on the wreck. He saw movement on board and swam through the waves to rescue the captain's wife. He tied her to himself and swam ashore with her. His heroism was recognised by an award from the Royal National Institution.*

Standing on the cliffs just before you reach the teashop is the old church of

The Yealm estuary.

Wembury dedicated to St Werburgh. There has been a church here since Celtic times though the present building mainly dates from the 14th and 15th centuries. It is a bit of a mystery why a church in Devon should be dedicated to St Werburgh since she had no known connection with the county. She was the daughter of Wulfhere, the first Christian king of Mercia, and spent much of her life in Ely convent in East Anglia. Her body, after being disinterred and moved several times, finally came to rest in Chester cathedral where a magnificent shrine was erected and still stands. The church is well worth a visit and there is comprehensive information available inside.

6. After tea, turn left and cross the stream by a wooden bridge. Immediately over the bridge turn right through a gate and follow a path to a road.

7. Take the public footpath signed for Ford opposite the junction. Bear left after 40 yards. This is an actively used bridleway so use the permissive path alongside, which has many seats.

8. At a lane turn right. At Wembury Square continue in the same direction, signed 'Plymstock', back to the start.

Walk 3
LODDISWELL AND THE AVON VALLEY

This walk is a cocktail of the best countryside South Devon has to offer - rolling scenery with extensive views, woodland and riverside paths and a visit to an attractive village nestling into a south facing hillside.

The Mill Coffee Shop is located in a lovely setting in an old corn mill on the river Avon and is now surrounded by a garden centre. It serves scrumptious cakes and cream teas and has some tables outside. It is open every day except Tuesday. On weekdays it opens between 10.30 am and 5 pm and on Sundays between 2 pm and 5 pm, all through the year except January. Telephone: 01548 550066.

DISTANCE: 5 miles.

MAP: OS Landranger 202 Torbay and South Dartmoor.

HOW TO GET THERE: From Sorley Green Cross on the A381 Totnes to Kingsbridge road take the road signed 'Loddiswell'. At Rake Cross bear right, signed

'Woodleigh 1½' and 'Preston 3' and park in one of the two laybys on the left after ½ mile.

STARTING POINT: Laybys on the road by the river Avon (GR 724481).

ALTERNATIVE STARTING POINT: The teashop is very close to the end of this walk and the recommended starting point is the nearest place that a car can be left for a long period. If you want to have tea before setting off, continue along the road then take the first lane on the left. The garden centre containing the teashop will be found a little way ahead on the right.

THE WALK

1. Walk along the road with the river on your right. At the bridge at New Mill do not cross the bridge but take an initially overgrown path on the right to continue on the river bank. Follow this path up some stone steps, across a lane and down some more steps on the other side. Do not go over the stile ahead but walk along the right-hand side of the field by the river.

2. Cross a plank bridge and stile on the right to stay by the river and then look for a wooden bridge half-left in the field and use this to cross a tributary. Continue ahead to the right-hand end of the field, keeping left to avoid mud.

3. Cross the stile onto a lane and turn right. At a road junction at Culverwell Bridge after 40 yards bear right. Walk along the lane as far as the next bridge over the river.

4. Immediately over the bridge take a track on the right. Watch for a slightly obscure stone stile on the right. Over this the path lies across the fields but is often not visible on the ground. To begin with it goes diagonally left across the field to a gate in the top corner. Its route is along the left-hand side of the next field to a gate in the top corner, straight across the middle of the next field and then in the same direction along the right-hand side of three more fields, emerging on a lane at a bend.

From this path there are extensive views across the rolling Devon countryside. This area is called South Hams. The name is very ancient: as far back as AD 846 King Aethelwulf granted land in 'South Hammes'. The name means enclosed or sheltered place and this favourable climate has led to the successful development of a vineyard a couple of miles north of Loddiswell.

5. Continue walking in the same direction along the lane into Loddiswell. At a T-junction by the school turn left and at the next junction continue in

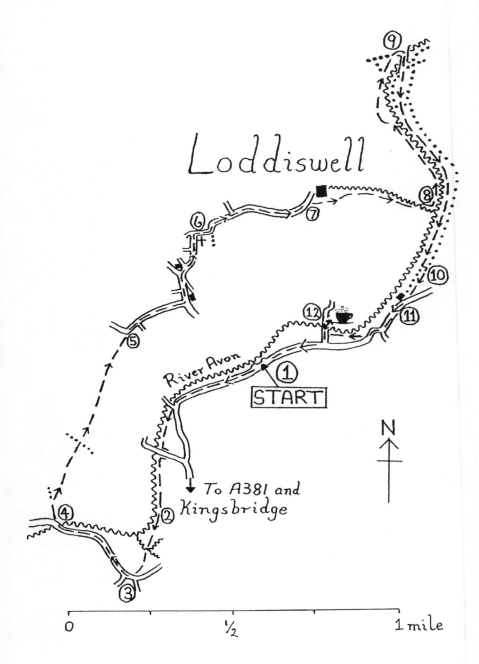

Loddiswell

START

River Avon

To A381 and
Kingsbridge

N

0   ½   1 mile

the same direction. Pass to the right of the Loddiswell Inn and immediately bear right to walk to the church.

6. Take the lane to the left of the church. At a junction continue ahead on a lane signed 'Reads Farm only'.

7. Just before the farm take a public footpath on the right and follow a charming path by a stream as far as the bank of the river.

8. Turn left and follow the path along the river bank.

The river Avon does not have far to flow to the sea from where it rises at Avon Head on Dartmoor and in that distance it falls some 1,500 feet. This means it is fast flowing and acidic because it rises among the moorland peats. These are ideal conditions for brown trout which can often be seen lurking, waiting to dart out to catch a tasty morsel. In the past there were lots of salmon too. The 11th-century residents of Loddiswell had to pay their Lord of the Manor 30 salmon a year for the privilege of catching them.

9. After about ½ mile turn right on a cross-path and then shortly up some steps onto an old railway bridge over the river. Turn right to cross the river. There is a maze of paths just here. Take the wide, main path ahead.

This is the route of the old railway between South Brent and Kingsbridge. It was one of the most beautiful stretches in the country and was aptly called the Primrose Line. It fell to the Beeching axe in 1963 but now this path follows its course so we can enjoy its beauties. In the spring it is brilliant with flowers - snowdrops, wild daffodils, wood anemones and bluebells in their season. The best time to see the primroses is in March, most years.

10. At a gate across the track, go over a stile on the left to join a path you may have noticed running parallel with the route for some way. Continue in the same direction to the road by the old Loddiswell station, now a house.

11. Turn right along the road. Shortly after a railway bridge over the road, go through a gate on the right to join a path once more along the river bank. At a lane turn right over the bridge to the teashop in the garden centre.

12. After tea, return to the lane and turn left. At a T-junction turn right, back to the start.

21

Walk 4
BOLT HEAD

Spectacular cliffs make this an exceptionally beautiful and interesting walk - and on a sunny day with brilliant yellow gorse, blue sky and sparkling sea this is a magical place. The climax of the walk is Overbecks Garden and museum, beautifully tended by the National Trust.

The teashop at Overbecks Garden is on the terrace and has stunning views. The house is shared with the Youth Hostel and teas are served in the dining room or can be taken outside. Because the kitchen is shared, the range offered is limited to some excellent cakes and no cream teas. It is open from the beginning of April to the end of October every day except Saturday between 12 noon and 4.15 pm. If you feel you must have a cream tea and are not a member of the National Trust and do not want to pay to go in the garden, Bolt Head Hotel nearby serves cream teas between March and November. Telephone: Overbecks 01548 842893. Bolt Head Hotel 01548 843751.

When Overbecks and the Bolt Head Hotel are closed, an alternative source of refreshment is the Tides Reach Hotel at South Sands, about ¼ mile off the route. This luxurious hotel has a sun lounge with plate glass windows overlooking the bay and serves excellent teas. It is open from February until December but it is best to check the exact dates (01548 843466).

DISTANCE: 4 miles.

MAP: OS Landranger 202 Torbay and South Dartmoor.

HOW TO GET THERE: Take the A381 Salcombe road from Kingsbridge. At Malborough follow the road called Higher Town, signed 'Village Centre, Galmpton, Hope Cove, Soar and Bolberry'. Continue on this road out of Malborough and ignore all roads to the right. Ignore the first road on the left after leaving Malborough and then shortly bear left, leaving the 'main' road. Continue on this for ½ mile, ignoring a road on the right, to a car park.

STARTING POINT: The car park near Higher Soar (GR 713376).

ALTERNATIVE STARTING POINT: If you want to visit the teashop at the beginning or end of your walk, start at Overbecks Garden where there is ample parking in the National Trust car park. The teashop is in the garden. You will then start the walk at point 5.

THE WALK

1. Leave the car park by continuing along the lane by which you reached it. After about 100 yards, turn right on a signed footpath, opposite a brick hut. Follow the path to a farm, ignoring a path on the right. Pass the farm and continue along the right-hand side of a field to a gate.

2. Immediately through the gate turn left. The path is not always visible on the ground but follows the line of a wall on the left. When the path reaches the cliff edge cross a stile by a gate and continue on the cliff edge, bearing right to a gate. Do **NOT** go straight ahead to a stile with a signpost. Follow the main path as it follows the cliff edge to a stile.

3. Over the stile bear slightly right towards a wartime lookout and again continue along the cliff edge. There are superbly placed seats from which to admire the magnificent views. As you turn the corner into the river estuary the vegetation changes dramatically and the path passes through mixed woodland carpeted with bluebells, primroses and wild garlic in spring.

The first bay after rounding Bolt Head is Starehole Bay. Sometimes, through the clear water, the remains of the Finnish barque Herzogin Cecilie *can be seen. This*

23

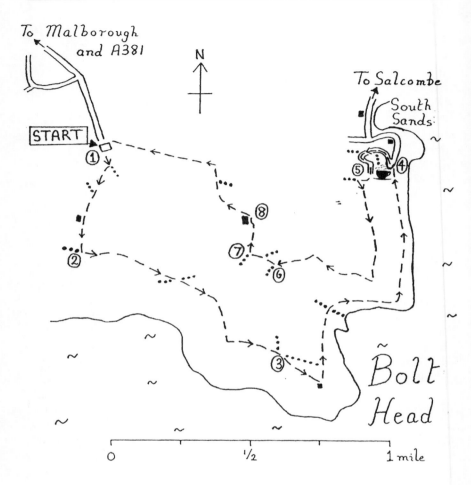

To Malborough and A381

N

To Salcombe

South Sands

START

① ② ③ ④ ⑤ ⑥ ⑦ ⑧

Bolt Head

0   ½   1 mile

foundered on the nearby Hamstone in 1936. It was hoped to salvage her and she was towed round to Starehole Bay but further storm damage put an end to that plan. Before she finally sank the rotting cargo of grain could be smelt for miles and thousands came to see her.

4. At the road turn left and follow the drive up to the gardens and museum. (To go to the Bolt Head Hotel for tea, turn right for a couple of hundred yards. On leaving the hotel, retrace your steps to where the coast path joined the road and continue up the drive to the entrance to the garden and museum. At the entrance turn right on the upper cliff path. To visit the

Tides Reach Hotel continue down the road towards Salcombe for about 300 yards and then retrace your steps to rejoin the main route.)

Overbecks garden and the present house on this site both date to the early years of the 20th century. It gets its name from Otto Overbeck, a larger than life character who bought it in 1928. He was a research chemist from Grimsby of Dutch extraction. He invented non-alcoholic beer, and an electrical rejuvenator which claimed to cure 'all illnesses ... with the exception of malformation and germ diseases'. The museum in the house has a varied collection reflecting Overbeck's wide interests and the time during the First World War when it was used as a convalescent home. Overbeck left the property to the National Trust in 1937 as a park, museum and for youth and most of the house is used as a youth hostel. It is the garden that steals the show. Backed by woodlands and cliffs it has an extremely mild climate and can grow a wide range of less hardy and exotic plants. The formal garden has a bronze statue of a girl called First Flight *and is a blaze of colour in summer. The views across the Salcombe estuary are stunning: a place to linger!*

5. Return to the entrance and turn left on the upper cliff path. At a path junction by the National Trust collecting box turn left, signed 'Sharp Tor', up some steps. Continue on the path, passing Sharp Tor trig point.

6. Shortly after the path starts to descend watch for a path over a stile on the right signed 'Soar Mill Cove'. Over the stile, head for a signpost straight ahead. At the signpost turn left on an unsigned path.

7. After 100 yards, just before a gate, turn right on a path signed 'Malborough and Soar Farms'. The path is not always visible on the ground but heads along the left-hand side of two fields to a stile by a gate at East Soar Farm.

8. Over the stile, join the farm track ahead, back to the car park.

Walk 5
PRAWLE POINT AND EAST PRAWLE

Prawle Point is the most southerly point of Devon and has very different scenery to the east and west of it. The walk starts along the low cliffs to the east and these give easy access to the shore, which is a rocky, wave-cut platform. These are splendid places for looking at the fascinating life found on rocks between high and low water. Children from five to ninety-five can spend an enjoyable hour fossicking about on the shore but to make the most of this it is important to choose a day when it will be low water about the time you plan to start the walk. The route then climbs to East Prawle for tea and returns by the more rugged cliffs to the west of Prawle Point.

Grunters café in East Prawle looks like a modern building but in fact it is housed in a restored potato barn, as a careful inspection of the walls of the adjacent shop will show. It is an unpretentious establishment but the scones are truly excellent. It is open every day from the beginning of April to the end of September between 9 am and 6 pm on weekdays and 11 am and 6 pm on Sundays. There are some seats outside. Telephone: 01548 511486.

When the teashop is closed, an alternative source of refreshment on this walk is the Pigs Nose Inn opposite, which serves lunches and evening meals.

DISTANCE: 5 miles.

MAP: OS Landranger 202 Torbay and South Dartmoor.

HOW TO GET THERE: From the A379 some 4 miles east of Kingsbridge take the road signed 'East Prawle'. Continue through the village, past the village green, to the National Trust car park at Prawle Point.

STARTING POINT: The National Trust car park at Prawle Point (GR 775354).

ALTERNATIVE STARTING POINT: If you want to visit the teashop at the beginning or end of your walk, start in East Prawle where there is space to leave a car by the village green. The teashop overlooks the green. You will then start the walk at point 5.

THE WALK

1. Start over the stile and down the steps by the National Trust collection box and go straight ahead to reach the coast path. Turn left. After about a mile the path reaches a track. Turn left (right leads down to the shore) and then shortly right to continue on the coast path for about a further mile.

Along this path there are many spots where it is easy to get down onto the shore. At low tide an extensive wave-cut platform is exposed and this is an ideal spot for looking at the shore life. The organisms which live on a rocky shore such as this have to survive in an incredibly difficult environment. They are alternately exposed to desiccation when the tide is out and then are covered with water. They are basically sea animals adapted to life in salt water but are flooded with fresh water when it rains. When the tide is in they are eaten by creatures from the sea such as crabs and when the tide is out they are the prey of sea birds. This is why so many of the animals have a protective shell.

2. The path turns inland and, at a right-hand bend, take a path on the left signed 'Woodford 3/4'.

3. Almost at the top of the hill turn left on a public bridleway signed 'East Prawle 3/4'. Join a track and turn right. At the second right-hand bend turn left on a public bridleway signed 'East Prawle 1/2', going through the left-hand gate. Follow the clear path along the right-hand side of the field, down

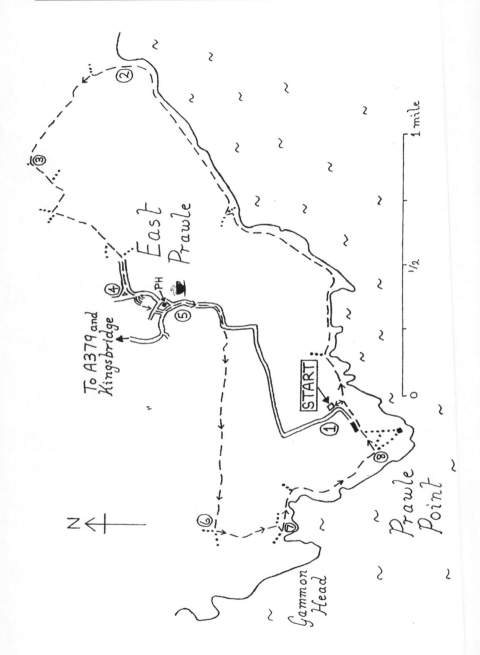

into a dip, up the other side and along a track, ignoring tracks to the right and left. Continue ahead as the track becomes a lane.

4. At a T-junction turn left and then almost immediately right by an electricity sub-station. Opposite some garages take a path marked by yellow arrows between a hedge and fence to emerge at a road. Go straight ahead and then left at the T-junction. The teashop is on the left, across the village green, in 100 yards.

There have been many shipwrecks on this part of the coast. In 1872 the survivors of an Italian wreck were staying at the village inn. In a violent argument one of the seamen stabbed three of his shipmates. He then stabbed a coastguard, who had been called to the incident because there was no policeman, and escaped to the coastguard cottages we pass later in the walk. There he stabbed another officer and his wife before being overcome and sustaining injuries from which he eventually died.

5. From the teashop cross the village green to return to the road and turn left. At a left-hand bend, by the entrance to Ash Park, turn right on a public bridleway signed 'Gammon Head 1'.

This track, parallel with the sea, is about 400 feet above sea level. It is on an old wave-cut platform and there are cliffs to the right. You may have noticed a similar phenomenon near the start of the walk. During an Ice Age the sea level falls because so much water is locked up in ice. As the ice melts the sea level rises again and these old cliffs and platforms are evidence of sea levels millions of years ago. The sea level is still rising after the last Ice Age which ended only (!) 10,000 years ago.

This area is very popular with bird watchers. There are many sea birds to be seen and this is often the first landfall for birds migrating north. More amazing still are the migratory butterflies - red admirals, clouded yellows and painted ladies - which can sometimes be seen arriving at the end of their journey, some from as far as North Africa.

6. Turn left at a cross-path after $3/4$ mile. Follow this to the clifftop coast path, ignoring a path on the left as it zigzags down.

This stretch of coast has been the graveyard of many ships and stories of shipwrecks abound, often caused by wind and waves but sometimes by human hand. In 1915 HMS Formidable *was torpedoed. In one of the boats which they managed to launch before she sank were 60 survivors and the ship's dog. One man was thought to have died of exposure and put to one side, covered in sacking. The dog curled up to sleep on the sacking and the warmth of its body revived the man. The wreck you can see rusting away at the bottom of the cliff is the remains of the* Heye P, *a 300 ton coaster wrecked in 1979. All the crew were safely lifted off by helicopter.*

Gammon Point, the promontory just to the right of where you rejoin the coast path and where two Spanish galleons sank after the Armada, is thought by many to be the most photogenic in Devon. The attractive little beach just by it is called Maceley Cove. Atlantic grey seals can sometimes be seen here.

7. Turn left along the coast path.

8. Immediately after a stile turn left, passing some cottages, once providing homes for the coastguards. When you reach the point where you joined the coast path, turn left and retrace your steps back to the start.

It is worth diverting from the route after the stile and going straight ahead to the white lookout station which can be seen on the cliffs. This is Prawle Point and it commands wide sea views. The name comes from the Saxon Prawbyll. Praw means to peep or look so this has obviously been a lookout for over 1,000 years. The building was originally a Lloyd's signal station with a telegraph connection to Lloyd's in London to send news of shipping.

Walk 6
DARTMOUTH CASTLE

This is a short and energetic walk along the cliffs, returning through National Trust woodland. Although the cream teas are delicious, it might be wise not to over indulge as the return leg of this walk has a sharp climb after tea. If you do have a substantial tea, be sure to spend plenty of time standing and staring and enjoying the magnificent views!

Dartmouth Castle tea rooms, next to the castle, serve cream teas and a selection of delicious home-made cakes. There are no seats outside but you will find plenty of benches around to which you can carry your tea (though no pots are allowed outside). The teashop is open between 10.30 am and 5 pm, from Easter to the end of September and again for the October half term. Telephone: 01803 833897.

When the teashop is closed, there are no alternative sources of refreshment on the walk itself. The nearest are in Dartmouth, a good ½ mile away along the road, where there are several teashops.

DISTANCE: 3 miles.

MAP: OS Landranger 202 Torbay and South Dartmoor.

HOW TO GET THERE: From the A381 Totnes to Kingsbridge road take the A3122 (this used to be the B3207) towards Dartmouth. On the outskirts of Dartmouth turn right on the A379, Yorke Road, signed for Stoke Fleming, Strete and Blackpool Sands. In about a mile, at a complex junction with a house on an island, take the next left, unsigned. Follow this over a crossroads to a car park.

STARTING POINT: Little Dartmouth car park (GR 874492).

ALTERNATIVE STARTING POINT: If you want to visit the teashop at the beginning or end of your walk, start at Dartmouth Castle where there is a car park. The teashop is by the castle. You will then start the walk at point 6.

THE WALK

1. Leave the car park through a gate at the south end by a path signed 'Coast Path and Dartmouth'.

2. At the coast turn left along the main path with first a fence and later a wall on the left.

3. At the end of the wall go through the gate. After 10 yards bear left to stay on the upper path. Follow the clear path across a small bridge to a second gate and on along the cliffs.

4. After another gate bear right downhill when the path splits. By a seat continue downhill on a less obvious path in the direction shown by an arrow on a post. Continue on round the coast, through further gates and soon Kingswear Castle across the estuary comes into view.

The cliffs in this area all belong to the National Trust. They were bought with Enterprise Neptune funds, a local appeal and a donation from the Devon Federation of Women's Institutes to mark their Golden Jubilee. In 1860 one of the first submarine cables was laid from Compass Cove to Guernsey, a feat presently commemorated by a sign.

☕ **5.** The path joins a lane by a house. This lane leads down towards Dartmouth Castle but walking on the road can be avoided by turning right in 20 yards and taking the lower of the two paths. Ignore a path on the right going steeply downhill and continue ahead, returning briefly to the wall by the road, and then branching right away again. Bear left by a brick hut to rejoin the road. After 20 yards turn right down some steps by some railings to Dartmouth Castle and the tea rooms.

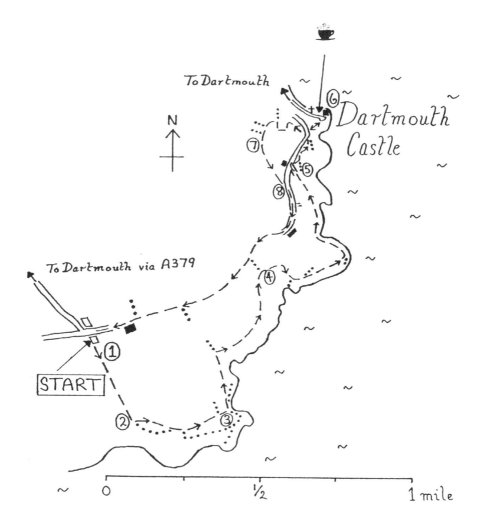

Dartmouth has a large deep water harbour and is difficult to detect from the sea. It grew in importance after the Norman Conquest when William's supporters, given lands in the area, found it a convenient port for keeping in touch with their continental properties. In the 12th century fleets setting out on both the Second and Third Crusades assembled here.

The behaviour of maritime traffic in the Middle Ages would be termed piracy today: capture or sinking of foreign merchants' ships (or sometimes those of rival fellow countrymen) was considered fair game. The Dartmouth captains were particularly notorious and this, combined with the skirmishes of the Hundred Years War, made the burghers of Dartmouth feel nervous. Following a French raid a fort was built in 1388. At this time John Hawley was mayor of Dartmouth. A colourful and charismatic character (with dubious business morals?), he is said to be the model of Shipman in Chaucer's Canterbury Tales. *The ruins by the car park are the remains of this fort.*

The castle we see today was started in 1481 and was the first designed for guns with gunports which covered the estuary rather than modified arrow slits. As an extra defence a companion castle at Kingswear on the opposite bank of the estuary was started in 1491 and a chain could be stretched between them. The castle was extended and modified in the succeeding centuries and was last used as a gun emplacement and lookout post in the Second World War. The lookout pill box was decorated with rough crenellations to look at first glance like part of the ancient castle. Part of the D-Day invasion fleet assembled at Dartmouth. The castle is now in the care of English Heritage and is open to the public every day between 10 am and 6 pm from the beginning of April to the end of October and on Wednesday to Sunday between 10 am and 4 pm in the winter (Telephone: 01803 833588).

The church near the castle is dedicated to St Petrox. He was a Celtic saint who is supposed to have had a cell here. He died in about AD 594 and was buried at Bodmin. In 1177 his body was stolen by monks from the monastery at St Meen in Brittany. The prior of Bodmin appealed to the King, Henry II, and on his orders an armed body of men compelled the abbot to surrender the corpse. The relics were taken to the King at Winchester and then to Bodmin where the casket which contained them still exists. We do not know exactly the route they took but as Dartmouth was then one of the principal ports for Brittany it is possible that the relics landed here. There is much more information about the church available within.

6. From the tea rooms retrace the route up the steps to the road and take a path opposite into Gallant's Bower. This climbs in a zigzag with one left-hand bend followed by two right-hand bends. Some 25 yards after the second right-hand bend take a path on the left to climb the hill. At the top bear left and ignore paths on the right except to visit the remains of the Civil War fort.

At the outbreak of the Civil War Dartmouth Castle was fully commissioned because of the danger of attack by pirates. The town declared for Parliament but was captured for the Royalists by Prince Maurice after a short siege. A garrison was stationed in Dartmouth Castle and an extensive earthwork fort built on top of Gallant's Bower. The Royalists, commanded by Sir Hugh Pollard, put up little resistance and Dartmouth Castle and the fort on Gallant's Bower quickly fell to the

Parliamentary forces when they attacked Dartmouth in 1646. At the end of the Civil War the 'new fort' on Gallant's Bower was demolished. The hill is wooded today but it still has fine views. The tapering structure on the hill top across the river beyond Kingswear Castle is a Day Mark built in the 1860s by the Harbour Commissioners to help with navigation. As you look upriver, the Royal Naval College can be seen.

7. Follow the thankfully now level path through the wood to a lane.

8. Turn right. Pass behind some houses and continue ahead in the same direction through a gate on a clear path. Go straight on through a gate when the path becomes an unsurfaced track and follow this through Little Dartmouth Farm back to the car park.

The river Dart.

Walk 7
BRIXHAM

This walk combines an easy cliff walk with exploring the fascinating old fishing port of Brixham. The cliff walk involves remarkably little climbing and has some splendid views across St Mary's Bay and Torbay. It visits Berry Head which has old forts, a lighthouse and large seabird colonies as well as a teashop and it is worth allowing plenty of time to explore.

 The teashop at Berry Head is in the old guard house of the northern fort. It serves cream teas and a range of home-made cakes and is particularly noted for its apple cake which is deliciously moist and spicy. The teashop is open from Easter to the beginning of October from 11 am to 5 pm every day, extending to 10 am to 6 pm in high season. Telephone: 01803 882678.

When the teashop is closed, there are several alternative sources of refreshment in Brixham. Spinnakers, passed on the route at point 9, serves excellent teas and is open on Friday, Saturday and Sunday in winter as well as the rest of the week in the season (Telephone: 01803 852121).

DISTANCE: 3¹/₂ miles.
MAP: OS Landranger 202 Torbay and South Dartmoor.
HOW TO GET THERE: In Brixham follow the signs for the central car park. If you
are coming from Torquay, an alternative is to travel to Brixham by the ferry
which runs during the summer season. From the ferry walk up Middle Street and
the central car park is on the left.
STARTING POINT: Central car park, Brixham (GR 924561).
ALTERNATIVE STARTING POINT: If you want to visit the teashop at the beginning
or end of your walk, start at Berry Head where there is a large car park. The
teashop is in the northern fort, signed from the car park. You will then start the
walk at point 6.

THE WALK

1. Leave the car park at the south-west end, the furthest away from the
harbour, and turn left down Union Lane. Turn right along Fore Street. At the
traffic lights turn left along Bolton Street and carry on across the traffic lights
at Rea Barn Road where the road changes its name to Greenswood Road.
After 170 yards turn left along Castor Road and then left again up Penn
Lane.

2. Turn right along Briseham Road and after 50 yards turn left on a signed
public footpath by a house called The Nook. The path passes the back of
houses and emerges in a field. Bear left. At the far end of the field, in front
of a wall, bear left again and follow this path, ignoring all side paths on the
left, to emerge on a road in front of the entrance to St Mary's Bay Holiday
Village.

3. Cross the road and continue ahead on a signed path. After 25 yards
follow the path round to the right and in a further 20 yards, after a stile, turn
left on a path signed 'Berry Head'.

4. At the clifftop, by a railing where a path leads down to St Mary's Bay,
turn left along the clifftop. Follow this path for about a mile to Berry Head
Country Park. There are some seats very well placed for admiring the
superb views of the cliffs at greater leisure.

5. On entering Berry Head Country Park the path splits. Take the
right fork, signed 'Coast Path via Fort', and follow the path, indicated by
acorns, round to the left of the southern fort. The southern fort can be

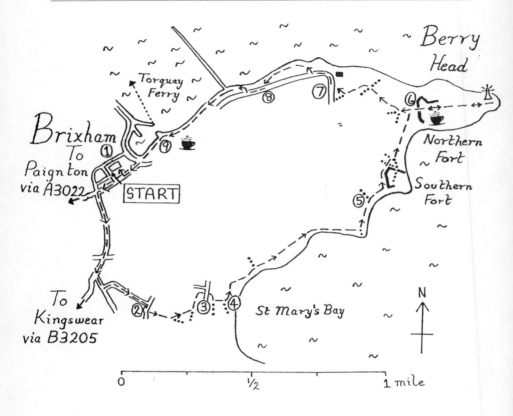

explored by turning right when the wall ends. Continue to the northern fort, seen ahead, by one of the several paths.

Berry Head is the southern tip of the pincers of land surrounding Torbay. It is a superb defensive position and has been fortified since the Iron Age. Berry is a corruption of Byri, the Saxon word for fortification.

When France declared war in 1793 some huts to house troops were built inside the 18 foot high Iron Age ramparts. Work started on more permanent forts in 1803. Three forts were planned but only two were built. The southern fort was number one, the northern fort was number three and they were built between 1803 and 1805. The planned site for number two was a little further round the headland and is passed later in the walk. The forts were never needed for defence, of course, and the closest Napoleon came was when the ship carrying him to St Helena, the HMS Bellerophon, *put into Torbay. The forts were abandoned in 1820-25 and the land sold. Various structures remain and plaques explain what can be seen. The guard house of the northern fort houses the teashop. Originally two rooms fronted by a veranda, it was extended to its present shape in 1906 and a new roof was added to protect the old one which still remains beneath. During the Second World War there was renewed endeavour here with various gun emplacements and observation posts.*

Within the northern fort is Berry Head lighthouse. It is sometimes said to be the lowest, highest and smallest lighthouse in Britain. On top of Berry Head it is 191 feet above sea level and there is none higher; being built so high the structure itself does not need to be very tall so it is the lowest.

Berry Head is now a country park, having been bought by Torbay District Council. It is also a Site of Special Scientific Interest. This is because the limestone rock and poor soil support an abundance of wild flowers including many rarities, so visitors are asked to admire but not to pick. On the cliffs are colonies of seabirds such as kittiwakes and fulmars. On the cliffs beneath the southern fort there is a large colony of guillemots; one of the few that is increasing in size.

6. From the northern fort entrance follow the surfaced track ahead for 100 yards. Turn right, signed 'Brixham'. When the tarmac surface ends continue on the main coast path, eventually bearing right down some steps to a lane.

7. Turn right along the lane. Immediately after passing between gate posts turn right through a car park and then left on a path by the shore. This eventually rejoins the road.

Berry Head Hotel was built in 1809 as the garrison hospital. Later it was the home of Reverend Henry Francis Lyte who wrote the hymn Abide With Me.

8. Turn right for 150 yards. Immediately after a small walled garden on the right, turn right down some steps to reach the shore again. Cross the shingle to the Breakwater Beach café and go ahead across the car park to join a path past the lifeboat station and the marina.

9. Follow round the harbour then turn left up Fore Street. Turn right down Union Lane back to the car park.

Brixham is caught between its past as a mighty fishing port and its present as a tourist resort. The fishing industry developed round a creek which is now largely filled in but originally extended about ½ mile inland from where today's inner harbour ends. The fishing industry based in Brixham was tremendously successful. One reason was that the fishermen who sailed from Brixham in the 18th century developed the technique of trawling involving dragging nets along the seabed. Fish from Brixham was exported all over the south-west and even to London, going by sea to Portsmouth and then overland. Changes in the fishing industry led to the decline of the fleet though there are still some inshore boats based in Brixham. This glorious past is commemorated in the various museums of the fishing industry in Brixham.

At the harbour are two monuments to significant moments in British history. The prominent statue is of William of Orange, later William III. It marks the spot where he landed to claim the throne of James II and launch the Glorious Revolution on 5 November 1688 with his famous declaration 'The Liberties of England and the Protestant religion, I will maintain'. In fact, what he is supposed to have said is 'Mine people, mine goot people, be not alarmed, I am come only for your good, **for all your goods***.' The small boat carrying him ashore got stuck in the mud and he was carried from it on the back of a local man.*

There is also a replica of the Golden Hind *permanently moored in the harbour. This was the ship which took Sir Francis Drake around the world between 1577 and 1580.*

The cliffs near Berry Head.

Walk 8
COCKINGTON

This walk starts, most unpromisingly, at Torbay gas works! However, do not let that put you off as this is a charming and easy stroll through woods and fields to the thatched village of Cockington. Considering how close it is to the bustle of Torquay and Paignton, it is remarkably quiet and you are unlikely to meet many other people (other than those clutching this book) except for the last half mile which uses the popular route to the village.

 The only problem you are likely to meet on this walk is the decision of where to take tea. The first teashop on the route is that in Cockington Court, which is now run as a craft centre. The tea room is open every day from 10 am to 5 pm. In the middle of the village itself is the Rose Cottage Tea Garden in the garden of a classic thatched cottage. This is open in the summer from Easter onwards between 10 am and 6 pm. However, if you can resist tea that long, Lanscombe House on the outskirts of Cockington is not to be missed. The dower house of Cockington Court, it was built in about 1730 and is supposed to be haunted but the present owner has never seen a ghost. It has a lovely sheltered garden in addition to tables inside and serves the usual teatime goodies as well as delicious fruit pies with clotted cream. Lanscombe House is open from mid March until the end of October between 10.30 am and 6 pm. Telephone: Cockington Court 01803 606035; Rose Cottage Tea Garden 01803 606607; Lanscombe House 01803 606938.

DISTANCE: 3½ miles (but you can do the final ½ mile by bus).

MAP: OS Landranger 202 Torbay and South Dartmoor.

HOW TO GET THERE: From Torquay take the coast road towards Paignton and ½ mile after the sign for Cockington Country Park watch for laybys on both sides of the road near the gas works.

STARTING POINT: Laybys on the coast road near Torbay gas works (GR 898625)

ALTERNATIVE STARTING POINT: If you want to visit the teashop at the beginning or end of your walk, start in Cockington where there is a car park. You will then start the walk at point 7.

THE WALK

1. Walk towards Torquay from the gas works and shortly take a path signed 'Mead Road' on the left. After 20 yards go through a gate to continue in the same direction. Stay on the main path through the wood to a road.

2. Turn left for 70 yards then right through a metal gate. Follow the path into and then along the valley, staying on the right-hand side of a stream and ignoring all side paths. Eventually the main stream diverges from the path which then soon comes to a lane.

3. Turn left. Opposite the entrance to Petersfield, turn right on a signed footpath through the first of two gates and follow the track to a farm.

4. Go through the gate and ahead to the left of farm buildings and then turn right between buildings on a signed footpath. This soon becomes a lane. When the lane takes a sharp left-hand bend, continue in the same direction across three fields on a signed public footpath.

At this point there is a panoramic view over Torquay and it is clear how close to the town this walk is, for all the route so far has been mainly through quiet woods (see walk 9).

5. The path now joins a designated horse riding route for 65 yards to a gate. Bear very slightly left to join a track with a hedge on the left and a wall

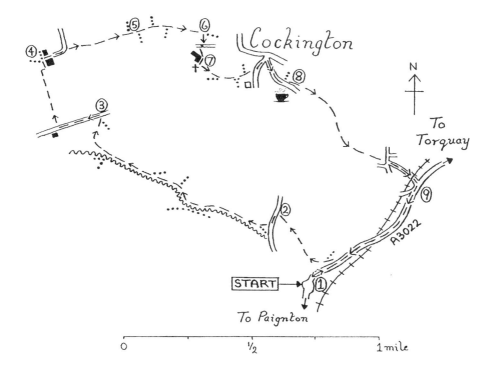

on the right. Ignore the first path on the right.

6. Take the second path on the right, which starts through a gap in the wall up six steps. Follow the path to a lane and turn right. After 25 yards turn left on a path signed 'Cockington Court'. This soon emerges on a tarmac drive at the side of Cockington Court. Walk round to the front of the building and the first opportunity for tea.

Cockington Court dates back to the 15th century though the Domesday Book refers to a prosperous Saxon manor here. The estate was sold in the 1920s to the Cockington Trust, dedicated to its conservation. Just before the war it was taken over by Torbay Borough Council and since 1991 has been managed as a country park. The house contains a craft centre as well as the tea room. The nearby church of St Mary and St George is worth a look, especially the screen and pulpit. The Renaissance pulpit is carved with cherubs bearing elephants' ears and rams' horns. A booklet available within contains a wealth of further information.

43

7. Follow the main drive away from Cockington Court. When this forks take the left branch to the road and turn left into the village. Rose Cottage Tea Garden is in front of you. Take the lane between this and the forge, passing Lanscombe House as you leave the village.

Cockington village is a perfectly preserved picture postcard village clustered round the famous thatched forge, timeless in spite of the modern buildings of Torquay lowering over it on the hills above. The most recent building is the Drum Inn, built in 1934 and carefully designed by Sir Edward Lutyens to fit into its surroundings. The village was bought by Prudential Insurance though most of the properties are now held on long leases.

8. Opposite Lanscombe House take a footpath on the left signed 'Sea Front' and follow the well-constructed path until it ends at a road and then continue in the same direction along Cockington Lane to the shore road.

9. Turn right, back to the start.

The walk along the sea front is not particularly interesting as you are mostly separated from the sea by buildings. There are very frequent buses along the road to the starting point so this bit of road walking can easily be avoided. The bus stop is a few yards to the right with seats looking out over the sea.

Walk 9
HOPE'S NOSE

This is an easy and exhilarating cliff walk which is very readily reached from the centre of Torquay. It also visits Kent's Cavern, an important archaeological site with guided tours, so allow plenty of time. After that, it is a gentle stroll back to the starting point.

The Pink Geranium Tea Room is a delightful classic teashop with a wide and tempting selection of delicious cakes and puddings as well as cream teas. It has smoking and non-smoking rooms and some tables outside in summer. The present owners do not know how it got its unusual name but try to live up to it with window boxes of geraniums in summer. The opening times are from 10.30 am to 5.30 pm every weekday except Saturday. On Sunday it is open for lunch at 12 noon with the regular menu available from 2.15 pm. Telephone: 01803 293862.

DISTANCE: 3 miles.

MAP: OS Landranger 202 Torbay and South Dartmoor.

HOW TO GET THERE: From Torquay harbour take the road signed 'Meadfoot and Babbacombe'. Turn right at the first set of traffic lights then bear left into Meadfoot Road. Follow this to Meadfoot beach.

STARTING POINT: Meadfoot beach. There is a car park at the east end of the beach or you may find some roadside parking (GR 936633).

ALTERNATIVE STARTING POINT: If you want to visit the teashop at the beginning or end of your walk, there is a large car park by the tea room at Kent's Cavern but this is for visitors to the caves. It might be possible to find a spot to park on the street in the vicinity. You will then start the walk at point 7.

THE WALK

1. Take the footpath from the car park signed 'Ansteys Cove'. At the road turn right. After ¼ mile, opposite a house called Compass South, take a footpath on the right signed 'Thatcher Point' and follow this along the cliffs until it rejoins the road.

It is very surprising to realise that this walk is in Torquay! Torquay has been recommended for bathing and summer visitors since the 18th century. During the Napoleonic War, the fleet was anchored in Torbay for long periods and officers' wives and families lodged ashore. Continental holidays were impossible then and so civilian visitors were also attracted by the mild climate. In particular, the medical officers with the fleet realised its benefits and began to recommend the resort to their private patients. Torquay thus gained a reputation as 'the town built to accommodate invalids'. In Victorian times there were special temperature controlled baths at the end of the pier for those not healthy enough to go into the sea itself. Its gentility so exasperated Rudyard Kipling he said it was 'a place as I do desire to upset it by dancing through it with nothing on but my spectacles'. It rightly remains a popular holiday destination despite the image given by the ghastly Basil Fawlty.

2. After 200 yards there is a path on the right that leads to the tip of Hope's Nose. It is well worth going along this for the views. After admiring the views, return to the road and take the signed 'Coast Path' opposite. Follow this path until it joins the road.

3. Cross the road and take a path directly opposite, signed 'Bishops Walk and Ansteys Cove'. After 45 yards turn left on the coast path.

4. The path splits shortly after rounding Black Head into Ansteys Cove. Take the left, upper, branch. Ignore another path on the right.

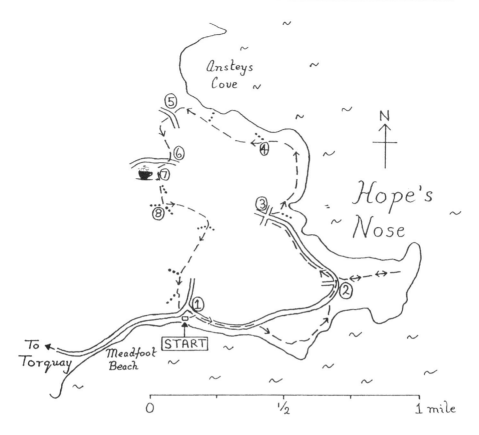

Ansteys (or Anstiss) Cove was a favourite destination of Victorian visitors to Torquay when apparently the following advertisement was to be seen:

PICNICS SUPPLIED WITH HOT WATER AND TEA
AT A NICE LITTLE HOUSE DOWN BY THE SEA;
FRESH CRABS AND LOBSTERS EVERY DAY,
SALMON PEEL, SOMETIMES RED MULLET AND GREY;
THE NEATEST OF PLEASURE BOATS LET OUT FOR HIRE,
FISHING TACKLE AS GOOD AS YOU CAN DESIRE;
BATHING-MACHINES FOR LADIES ARE KEPT,
WITH TOWELS AND GOWNS ALL QUITE CORRECT;
THOMAS IS THE MAN WHO PROVIDES EVERYTHING
AND ALSO TEACHES YOUNG PEOPLE TO SWIM.

5. Cross the lane and car park opposite and turn left to walk with the football pitch on your left and a wood on the right to a road.

6. Turn right to some steps on the opposite side of the road. The teashop is at the top.

The teashop is next to the entrance to Kent's Cavern, one of the most important sites of its kind in Europe and well worth visiting. There are guided tours which take about 45 minutes. Kent's Cavern was excavated by Father John MacEnery who was chaplain at Torre Abbey. He started in 1825, spending four years on excavations. He found thousands of bone fragments of long extinct animals such as mammoths and bison. After his death, his work was forgotten and it was not until 30 years later that he received recognition as a pioneer of scientific cave exploration. The work was continued by William Pengelly in 1865 who discovered a fragment of human bone embedded in a stalagmite. Flint spear heads and scrapers, a bone pin and harpoon heads show us something of the way of life of the people who lived in these caves 20,000 to 30,000 years ago but it is not known whether the caves were a permanent home or a seasonal refuge. Some of the finds can be seen at Kent's Cavern but many of the best are, of course, in Torquay Museum or the British Museum. The caves are open from 10 am every day. Telephone: 01803 294059.

7. From the teashop, turn right and walk in front of the entrance to Kent's Cavern to pick up a path at the far end, beyond the toilets. When the path splits after 30 yards, take the upper right branch.

8. At a cross-path 20 yards after joining a concrete drive, turn left. Follow this path, ignoring all paths on both left and right, until it starts to climb. At this point, in sight of the car park where the walk started, bear left onto a path to the car park and the start.

Walk 10
STOKEINTEIGNHEAD

If you feel that you have been over indulging in cream teas and need to burn off some calories so that you can enjoy some more, this is the walk for you! It is not very long but it starts with a switchback path along the cliffs before turning inland to the village of Stokeinteignhead and an outstanding teashop. The return to the starting point at Maidencombe is along an airy ridge. The magnificent views and a memorable tea will be ample reward for your efforts.

The Old Bakery is a superb traditional teashop. In addition to award winning cream teas with two sorts of jam, it serves delicious cakes and fruit crumbles. There are also some interesting suggestions for tea such as cheese with your scones. The building dates back to 1722 although the foundations and lower walls are believed to be 14th century. It was the village bakery between 1880 and 1950, from which it derives its name.

Outside there is a vine covered veranda with some tables. Telephone: 01626 873442.

When the teashop is closed, an alternative source of refreshment on this walk is the ancient Church Inn in Stokeinteignhead, across the road from the teashop, which serves excellent pub food.

DISTANCE: 5 miles.

MAP: OS Landranger 202 Torbay and South Dartmoor.

HOW TO GET THERE: From the B3199 Torquay to Teignmouth road 3 miles north of Torquay, take a minor road signed 'Maidencombe village ¼'.

STARTING POINT: The car park at Maidencombe (GR 927685).

ALTERNATIVE STARTING POINT: If you want to visit the teashop at the beginning or end of your walk, start in Stokeinteignhead where there are a few spots around the village where it is possible to park without causing inconvenience. The teashop is in the centre of the village. You will then start the walk at point 5.

THE WALK

1. From the entrance to the car park go along a track signed 'Labrador Bay and Teignmouth'. Ignore a signed footpath on the left and continue on the switchback path along the cliffs for a good mile. Take plenty of time to stand and stare and admire the view. Do not be misled by a sign proclaiming you have come 1½ miles from Maidencombe: it is rather exaggerated and either the person responsible for placing it could not measure distance or it was put in the wrong place.

2. Watch for a car park a field away on the left and shortly take a path over a stile on the left between a hedge and a wire fence.

3. At a road turn right for 250 yards then bear left on a minor road called Commons Lane.

4. At the top of the hill, just before the entrance to Fairhaven Farm, turn left on a hedged track. Bear left after about 300 yards when the track forks. Stokeinteignhead, nestling in the valley below, soon comes into view. At a lane turn right into the village. The teashop is on the right at a T-junction.

Stokeinteignhead is a charming village with many thatched buildings. Across the road from the teashop is the Church House Inn, which dates back to the 13th century. In 1993 the thatch caught fire and burned for 17 hours, devastating the first floor. It was rebuilt in the traditional style in cob by local craftsmen and

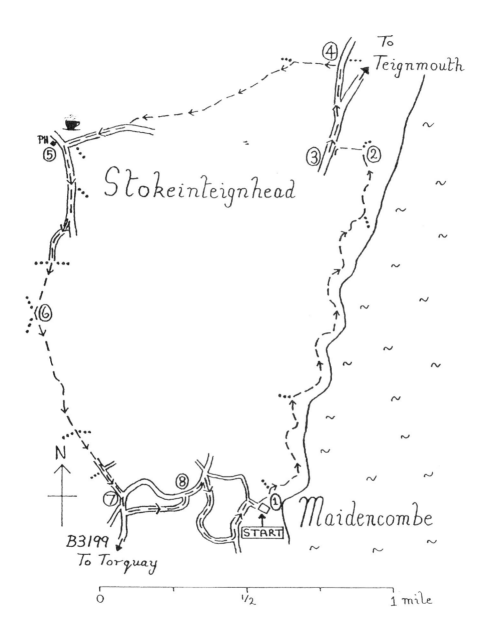

To Teignmouth

Stokeinteignhead

PH

N

B3199
To Torquay

Maidencombe

START

0   ½   1 mile

reopened eleven months later. Cob is a mixture including clay and straw brought to the right consistency by laborious treading, often carried out by cattle. It lasts a long time providing a good roof and a solid plinth keeps it dry. Damp makes the cob crumble and hence the Devon saying 'All cob wants is a good hat and a good pair of shoes'. Many buildings are lime washed in white, cream or other colours and the plinth of stone or rubble is coated in tar. This also discourages burrowing vermin.

5. From the teashop turn left along the road through the village. Bear right up a minor road by a thatched house called Tappers. This is little more than a track so the end of speed limit sign seems rather ironic. Continue ahead on the surfaced track at a cross-track by Pathways Nurseries.

6. At a complex junction of tracks turn left. Continue ahead at a cross-track and carry on as the surface improves, passing some houses.

7. Turn right at the main road and left along Sladnor Park Road after 50 yards.

8. Turn right at a T-junction and then right down Brim Hill. Turn left along Rock House Lane, back to the car park.

Rudyard Kipling and his wife Caroline moved to Rock House in 1896. They felt sure that the sunny aspect and nearby sea would provide the perfect conditions for writing. They stayed less than a year, discouraged by the 'spirit of deep, deep Despondency' which Kipling said the house possessed and made both him and his wife depressed. Nonetheless, he started work on several books during his time here including some 'parables on the education of the young' which were eventually published as Stalky and Co. in 1899.

Walk 11
DARTMEET

This is a delightful and easy walk on the banks of the East Dart, just above its confluence with the West Dart at Dartmeet. The return starts on the opposite bank but soon climbs the valley side to Brimpt's Farm for tea. It is a walk for fine weather, not because of the danger of losing your way but because you would be denied the wonderful panoramas that are such a feature in clear conditions. Also, you should not attempt it after very wet weather because it relies on crossing the river at some stepping stones.

 Brimpt's Farm is a 700 acre working farm that serves delicious cakes and scrumptious puddings as well as cream teas with hedgerow and blackcurrant jams. It prides itself on sensible British food at sensible prices and is open every day from March to October between 11 am and 6 pm. There is not much sign of tea as you approach the farm from the direction of this walk but have faith, go round to the front and you will be rewarded with an excellent repast! Telephone: 01364 631250.

When the teashop is closed the nearest alternative source of refreshment open all year is the Forest Inn at Hexworthy, a good ³/₄ mile off the route but clearly signed.

DISTANCE: 3¹/₂ miles.
MAP: Landranger 191 Okehampton and North Dartmoor.
HOW TO GET THERE: Follow the signs from the A38 near Ashburton or take the B3357 from Tavistock.
STARTING POINT: The car park at Dartmeet (GR 673733).
ALTERNATIVE STARTING POINT: There is no alternative starting point for this walk.

THE WALK

1. Take the public footpath signed 'Cater Gate and Sherril' at the far end of the car park, to the right of the entrance to the café. Join a path coming in from the right to continue in the same direction and ignore a grassy path soon joining on the right.

2. Follow the obvious path along the river until it ends at a tributary of the main river. This can be crossed by some quite tricky stepping stones. However, it is better to continue on the right-hand bank of the tributary for 300 yards to a clapper bridge.

Clapper bridges are the simple bridges made of slabs of stone found all over Dartmoor. They are not as ancient as their simplicity might suggest, mostly having been built after 1400 and some as recently as the first half of the 19th century.

3. Over the bridge turn left, back to the main river, and cross it by stepping stones.

4. Turn left. Start by walking back down by the river through woodland. When the path leaves the wood it begins to diverge from the river and runs close to a wall, on the right, to a tumbledown house.

The derelict house was an agricultural worker's cottage built in the 18th century and known as Dolly's Cot. Local legend has it that at one time it was lived in by orphans, a boy and a girl. The girl, Dolly, is said to have been very beautiful and was pursued by the Prince Regent when he was staying nearby. However, Dolly's head was not turned and she married a local lad from Hexworthy.

 5. After this, the path is much more obvious, up the side of the valley

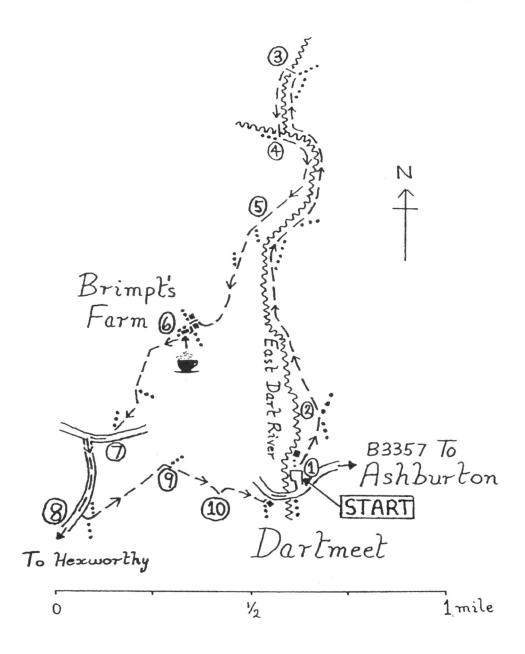

③

④

⑤

N

Brimpt's
Farm ⑥

East Dart River

②

⑦

⑨

B3357 To
Ashburton

①

START

⑧

⑩

Dartmeet

To Hexworthy

0   ½   1 mile

to the farm. Follow the signed path past farm buildings to the front of the white painted farm house and the entrance to the tea rooms.

6. After tea, leave along the concrete drive. When this bends sharply left, continue ahead on a track through the wood to a road.

7. Turn right. After 100 yards turn left on a lane signed 'Hexworthy'.

8. Opposite the entrance to Huccaby Farm, turn left on a track and after 40 yards turn left on a footpath signed 'Dartmeet'. Go through the gate and ahead across the field. The path is rather faint but its line is shown by yellow markers.

9. After the path makes a sharp right turn, stay on the path by the field boundary and then, after a stile, between walls.

10. At the end of the walls turn left and follow the yellow waymarks to some buildings at the bottom corner of the field. Go through a gate to the left of a cottage to a road. Turn right, back to the start.

The name Dartmeet refers to the confluence of the East and West Dart rivers just below the car park. The rivers rise a couple of miles apart on the boggy plateau of the moor. The East Dart leaves the high moor at Postbridge (see walk 12) and the West Dart at Two Bridges, both famous beauty spots. Just upstream from the road bridge are the remains of another clapper bridge, damaged by flood waters.

Walk 12
BELLEVER AND POSTBRIDGE

The first part of this varied walk is through Bellever Forest on well-made forestry tracks. There is an optional diversion of about a mile to the summit of Bellever Tor. This is not at all arduous. In fact, it is positively easy, being a climb of only about 100 feet, and it is strongly recommended for the superb panoramic views of Dartmoor. After visiting Postbridge and its famous clapper bridge, the return after tea is over open country with stunning moorland views all around. To enjoy this walk at its magnificent best, do be sure to choose a clear day.

The Lydgate House Hotel is in a wonderful position overlooking the East Dart valley. Teas are served in the conservatory and on the terrace, both with wonderful views, between 3 pm and 5.30 pm every day from April to the end of October. For a cream tea you can choose between white and brown scones and delicious cakes are also available. Telephone: 01822 880209.

When the teashop is closed, an alternative source of refreshment on this walk is the East Dart Hotel at Postbridge, on the main road, which serves food including, sometimes, teas with delicious cakes.

DISTANCE: 3½ miles with 1 mile optional extension.

MAP: OS Landranger 191 Okehampton and North Dartmoor.

HOW TO GET THERE: Take the B3212 Moretonhampstead/Two Bridges road to Postbridge and follow the signs for Bellever.

STARTING POINT: The Forestry Commission car park at Bellever (GR 656772).

ALTERNATIVE STARTING POINT: If you want to visit the teashop at the beginning or end of your walk, start in Postbridge where there is a large public car park at the National Park Information Centre. Starting at point 4, it is a short walk to Lydgate House Hotel. To visit the teashop after your walk, start at the main road in point 6 and continue on the public bridleway. Follow the directions given in point 4 to find the teashop when you have finished the circuit.

THE WALK

1. Return to the road and turn left. At a road junction go straight on. After the last building continue ahead on a track uphill.

Bellever Forest was planted in 1921 by the Duchy of Cornwall and bought by the Forestry Commission in 1931. The Forestry Commission was set up in 1919 to create a strategic reserve of timber to use as trench supports in another war. Conifers are very quick growing in the warm(!), wet British climate and so much of the planting was of sitka spruce and larch. The value of forests for recreation has been realised in more recent years as woods can absorb a lot of people without losing a sense of remoteness and the Forestry Commission now welcomes the public into its forests.

2. Immediately after a gate across the track, turn right. Continue across a forestry track to a complex junction of five paths and tracks.

The track you have walked up is the ancient coffin route to Lydford. Lydford parish extended over a huge area of Dartmoor and until the 13th century everyone who lived in the parish had to be taken to Lydford to be buried. It is called the Lich Way, meaning the road of the dead.

To visit Bellever Tor:
a) Continue in the same direction for 150 yards.
b) At a cross-path turn left and follow this to the summit of Bellever Tor.
c) After admiring the view, retrace your steps.

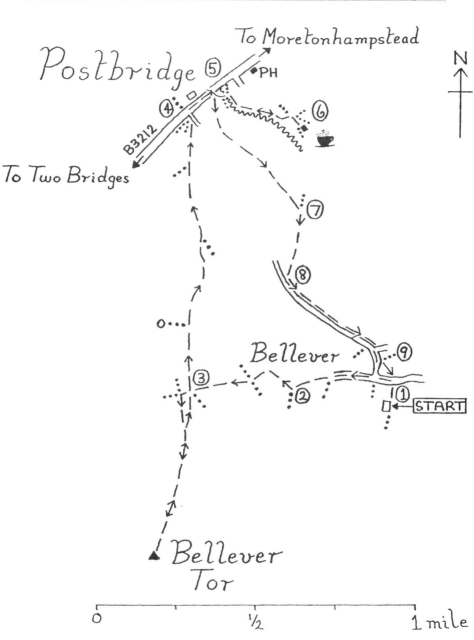

Postbridge ⑤

To Moretonhampstead

PH

B3212

To Two Bridges

⑥

⑦

⑧

④

Bellever

③

②

① START

⑨

▲ *Bellever Tor*

N

0   ½   1 mile

d) Just after a fallen wall, bear slightly right onto a path leading back to the junction mentioned above.

Bellever is one of the claimants to be the centre of Dartmoor. This tor, so easily reached, has outstanding views of the central moor stretching in all directions, including the famous and forbidding prison, seen in the distance. The number, size and arresting shapes of the tors are the feature that sets Dartmoor apart from many other areas of moorland in England. The granite core of Dartmoor was formed from molten rock welling up from deep in the Earth's crust. This pushed the layers of rock above up into a dome but did not break through and the rock therefore cooled slowly, forming large crystals. Eventually, the overlying layers were eroded away, exposing the granite to wind, water and ice. Much of the granite had been fractured and broken by the pressure from beneath and this allowed rain and wind to penetrate the rock and sculpt it into the fantastic shapes we see today.

3. Turn right. (Note: If you have been on the diversion up Bellever Tor, carry straight on.) Follow this track for about a mile to a lane.

Some 400 yards after the junction a short track on the left leads to a cairn circle and kistvaen or burial chamber. The Dartmoor we know today seems remote and wild: that is one reason why the prison is here. However, at the height of the Bronze Age, perhaps 1000 BC, the climate was rather more benign than it is today. In those days the area probably supported a population of about 7,000 people, more than it does at present. Life on the moor was probably easier than in dank, heavily wooded and often malarial valleys and the moorland forest was lighter and easier to clear. The moor we see today is largely the result of their labours: without human interference the area would be much more thickly wooded. Dartmoor therefore has an enormous concentration of ancient remains, built over a long time, of which this is just one example. Another reason why there seems to be such a concentration on Dartmoor is that any remains in the valleys are more likely to have been obliterated by more intense human activity since.

4. Turn left and then right along the B3212, passing a National Park Information Centre.

 5. Bear right to cross the river by the old clapper bridge then turn right along the river bank for 90 yards. Go through a gate on the left to continue along the river bank on a permissive path. The path eventually diverges from the river and climbs briefly by a fence to a track. Turn right to the hotel.

This clapper bridge is generally recognised as one of the best examples (see walk 11). It is almost certainly 14th century.

Around Postbridge a modern ghoul has come to frighten the unwary and the gullible! Just after the First World War there were a number of unexplained accidents on the road to the west of the village. These were blamed on a pair of mysterious hairy hands that wrenched the steering wheel or handlebars from the control of the owner. After a while they became less troublesome but then stories started of campers disturbed by scrabbling at the canvas ...

6. After tea, retrace your steps over the clapper bridge. Just as you rejoin the road take a public bridleway on the left, signed 'Bellever'.

7. At a cross-track turn right and continue along the track to a road.

8. Turn left and walk by the road into Bellever. The right of way is actually parallel with the road, a short distance to the left, but it is not at all apparent on the ground.

9. Just before a cattle grid bear left through a gate on a bridlepath. Cross the road, back to the start.

Walk 13
STICKLEPATH AND BELSTONE

This is a walk of stimulating contrasts. It starts in the village of Sticklepath where the Museum of Waterpower gives a fascinating glimpse of bygone technology. It is well worth a visit. The route to tea in the moorland village of Belstone is along the bank of the river Taw up Belstone Cleave and there are many delightful spots where you will be tempted to linger. Unusually for this book, the return leg after tea is perhaps slightly longer, as measured on the map, but it is very easy going along quiet field paths and tracks.

 The Barton in Belstone is a guest house and tea rooms offering teas every day throughout the year between 2 pm and 5.30 pm. The building is a traditional Devon longhouse, which dates from about 1670. There are plans to develop a museum here. It has a very attractive garden and serves delicious and substantial cream teas as well as a range of other teatime goodies. Telephone: 01837 840371.

DISTANCE: 4¹/₂ miles.

MAP: OS Landranger 191 Okehampton and North Dartmoor.

HOW TO GET THERE: Sticklepath is on the B3260 and is signed from the A30.

STARTING POINT: Finch Foundry, Sticklepath (GR 642941).

ALTERNATIVE STARTING POINT: If you want to visit the teashop at the beginning or end of your walk, start in Belstone where there is ample parking in the public car park on the edge of the village. Turn left out of the car park into the village and the Barton is at the far end of the village, on the left. You will then start the walk at point 6.

THE WALK

The force of the river Taw has been important to the village of Sticklepath, powering water wheels for various industries. Finch Foundry was established in 1814 on a site previously used for grinding corn and making woollen cloth. The name foundry is, strictly speaking, wrong. A foundry smelts metal from its ore and a forge makes objects from the metal so this was really a forge as it produced tools for agriculture and mining; it used to be said that Finch tools never wore out. The giant trip hammer and shears are still in working order, demonstrated by enthusiastic and knowledgeable guides. It is remarkable that what is essentially 18th-century technology was in commercial use until 1960. After the foundry closed, the machinery was preserved by a group of enthusiasts and taken into the care of the National Trust in 1993. A visit is strongly recommended. It is open from 1st April until the end of October every day except Tuesday, between 11 am and 5.30 pm (Telephone: 01837 840046).

The Quakers were an important part of the community and behind the foundry is the Quaker Burial Ground. It was bought for £14 by Tom Pearse, made famous with his grey mare in the song about Widecombe Fair. He was buried there in 1875. Tom Pearse also built the thatched summer house behind the foundry.

1. With your back to the foundry, turn right. Immediately after the bridge over the river turn right on a public bridlepath. (The same point can be reached from the back of the foundry by taking a path on the left between stone walls at the entrance to the car park from the garden. Follow the path round and cross the river by a wooden bridge and turn right.)

2. Some 20 yards after a gate across the track, turn right. Follow the delightful path by the river Taw, eventually crossing it by a footbridge.

3. Soon after the bridge, at a T-junction, turn left on a path signed 'Belstone and the moor'. Take the first path on the left to return to the river bank and continue upriver to recross it at a second footbridge. Over the bridge turn right to carry on upriver.

The river Taw is the boundary between the parishes of Belstone and South Tawton. The ceremony of beating the bounds takes place every seven years, for example in 1997 and 2004.

This path is part of a long distance footpath, the 180 mile Tarka Trail which explores the area that inspired the author Henry Williamson. Belstone Cleave features in his famous book, Tarka the Otter. *It is the scene of Tarka's fight with Swagdagger and the other stoats.*

4. This delightful path eventually deteriorates alarmingly and could even be dangerous for the less sure footed. This part should be avoided by bearing left to a higher level path. However, the start of the path is not easy to spot. It leaves the river bank path 70 yards after a short length of wall on the left. The river bank path then crosses a tiny stream and Belstone church comes into view. At this point there is a faint arrow on a rock showing the direction and a short climb soon reaches a good clear path. Continue towards Belstone, seen ahead. Should you miss this point, the river bank path eventually joins it but be warned, it is not easy walking!

Looking at the beautiful scenery, it is difficult to believe that this was once a mining area. Dartmoor is a huge mass of granite that welled up in a molten state from deep in the Earth, causing enormous heat and pressure in the surrounding rocks. Hot gases and fluids from this mass of granite, rich in many metals such as copper and lead, escaped into cracks in the surrounding rock. As they cooled they formed veins, which were mined millions of years later. For example, Ivy Tor mine on the left of the river was worked for copper on and off in the 19th century. There was another copper mine at Greenhill on the opposite bank of the river. The drainage was powered by a water wheel on the river Taw. This had a diameter of some 60 feet, the largest in Britain at the time.

5. Turn right at a T-junction with a wider path that leads down to the river. Cross the river at a footbridge and turn right and then left to follow the main path uphill. From this path there are wonderful views back down the Cleave. At a road turn left and then right. The teashop is on the first corner on the right.

6. From the teashop turn right and walk through the village, ignoring a road on the right signed 'Sticklepath'.

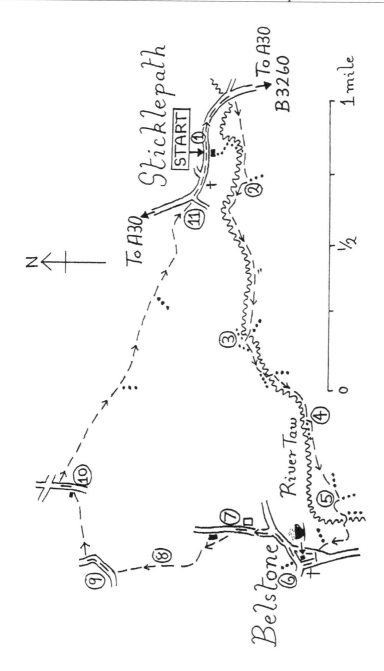

7. Some 200 yards after the village car park on the right, turn left in front of a house to a ladder stile. Bear left to a gate. Walk along the right-hand side of the field to another gate and the right-hand side of a second field until you approach the bank of a stream. Continue ahead with the stream on the left, keeping well to the left to avoid a boggy area.

8. Cross a stile into a wood and follow the path through the wood, crossing another stile, to emerge on a lane.

9. Turn right. About 40 yards after a left-hand bend take a public footpath on the right, signed 'Tongue End'. The path is not always visible on the ground. Head across three fields to a gate behind a building seen ahead. This is Tongue End Pumping Station.

10. Turn left along a lane. Turn right along a track crossing a cattle grid. Follow this track to Sticklepath, bearing left at a fork after another cattle grid and ignoring a footpath on the right.

The name Sticklepath comes from the Anglo-Saxon word 'stiegel' meaning steep. As you come down towards the village you will appreciate how this old packhorse route acquired its name.

11. Continue along the road into the village to the start, passing the church on the right.

Sticklepath was an industrial village and home to many Quakers. As such, it was somewhat neglected by the Church of England and the small church was a chapel of ease of Belstone church. The present building was erected in the 1870s to replace one that burned down. The Quakers of Sticklepath were the first people in Devon to welcome John Wesley as he tramped the country preaching Methodism. If you look back as you enter the village, a white-painted rock and flagpole mark the spot where he used to preach.

Walk 14
FINGLE BRIDGE

N̄o other walk in this book offers such a reward for so little exertion. It is true there is a climb to the famous Hunter's Path but it is quite gentle and your efforts will be rewarded by stunning views of the Teign Gorge. The walk can easily be done in an afternoon but you might want to consider making it into an all day expedition and including a visit to Castle Drogo, the last large country house to be built in England. After tea at the famous Fingle Bridge, the walk returns along the wooded banks of the river Teign.

 Fingle Bridge is the home of the Angler's Rest, a family run concern since its foundation as a tea shelter in 1897. It serves excellent teas as well as meals and has a bar. A terraced garden leads down to the river. It is open every day between 11 am and 5.30 pm from Easter to the end of September and in the winter the bar is open at lunchtime. Telephone: 01647 21287.

There is also a very good National Trust tea room at Castle Drogo.

DISTANCE: 4½ miles.

MAP: OS Landranger 191 Okehampton and North Dartmoor.

HOW TO GET THERE: Take the A382 from Moretonhampstead, signed 'Okehampton', towards the A30 at Whiddon Down. After 3 miles watch for a layby on the right-hand side of the road 200 yards north-west of the junction with the B3206 at Easton Cross.

STARTING POINT: The layby on the north east side of the A382, 3 miles north-west of Moretonhampstead (GR 716892).

ALTERNATIVE STARTING POINT: If you want to visit the teashop at the beginning or end of your walk, start at Fingle Bridge where there is a large public car park. You will then start the walk at point 9.

THE WALK

1. From the layby turn left towards Moretonhampstead. At Easton Cross turn left on a lane and continue for ¼ mile, ignoring a track and a public footpath on the left.

2. Immediately after a stone bridge over a stream, turn left on a path signed 'Fingle Bridge'. Follow the path round to the left, ignoring a path on the right at a bend after 80 yards and later a track over a bridge on the left.

As you walk along this path, Castle Drogo comes into view, perched high above the Teign Gorge on a well-chosen spur. It was the last 'castle' to be built in England; changing fashion, planning laws and the taxing away of family fortunes means that a grandiose showpiece like this is unlikely to be built again.

Sir Julius Drewe made his fortune from a grocery chain, the Home and Colonial Stores. He researched his family history and thought there was a connection between his family and a Norman, Drogo or Dru de Teigne, who gave his name to the village of Drewsteignton. He bought some land nearby and engaged Edward Lutyens to build a castle with all the comforts of the 20th century. Lutyens used the local granite from nearby quarries and the appearance of the castle reflects the ever changing weather, shining in the sun or glowering in the gloom.

3. Cross a stone stile in the wall on the left, signed 'Fingle Bridge', and follow the path to a metal footbridge over the river Teign. Over the bridge turn left for 15 yards then right on a path signed 'To Hunter's Path and road near Castle Drogo'. Follow this path to a lane.

This path is part of the Two Moors Way, which is a 100 mile walking route from the southern edge of Dartmoor at Ivybridge to the north coast of Exmoor at Lynmouth. It thus links the only two National Parks in south-west England and crosses them both

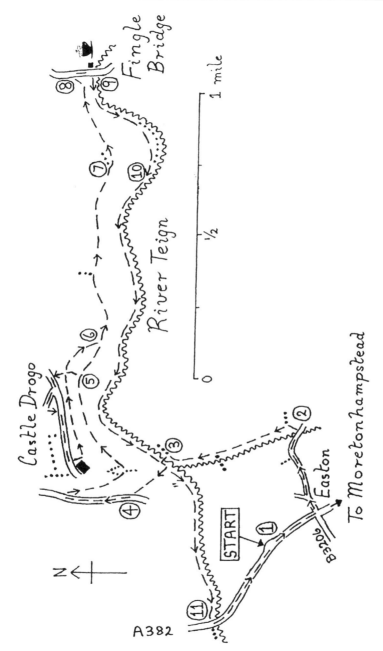

Fingle Bridge

Castle Drogo

River Teign

To Moretonhampstead

Easton

B3206

A382

START

N

0   ½   1 mile

north-south. The letters MW on signposts are waymarking for this route.

4. Turn right. After 300 yards turn right again on a path through a wooden gate, signed 'Hunter's Path'. Stay on the main path, soon passing a seat well placed to admire the views over the Teign Gorge.

5. To visit Castle Drogo:
   a) Take a signed path on the left up some steps.
   b) At a drive turn left and this leads to the castle and gardens.
   c) After your visit, take a path from the wide terrace in front of the castle, signed for the restaurant and lavatories to the left of the building. Go through a yew hedge and follow round to the left along the path signed 'Mr. Drewe's path' to rejoin the path up to the castle drive.
   d) Continue straight ahead at this point and the path soon leads down to rejoin the Hunter's Path further on, at point 6.

The building of Julius Drewe's romantic dream started in 1911. The original plan was for an even more ambitious structure but this was cut back soon after work started. Building progressed very slowly. Lutyens, as one of the leading architects of his day, was involved in numerous other commissions, including the government centre in New Delhi. Perhaps, too, Drewe lost some of his enthusiasm after his eldest

The old packhorse bridge over the river Teign.

son, Adrian, was killed in the First World War in 1917. One of the bedrooms was arranged as a memorial by his grieving mother. The building was only finished in 1930, a year before Julius Drewe died. In the gun room there is an interesting display of the plans and their changes as the project developed, together with contemporary photographs of the building work. The property was given into the care of the National Trust in 1974.

The house is fascinating to explore with many details showing how Lutyens tried to reconcile the quixotic ideal of a castle with the comforts of 20th-century life. For example, the radiators are concealed behind oak panels and the portcullis serves the dual purpose of letting air in while stopping the dog getting out. It is also worth taking time to enjoy the lovely gardens, which flourish protected by high yew hedges. These are intended to give the effect of a castle wall. Children will envy the charming Wendy house not far from the circular lawn.

Castle Drogo is open between 1st April and 31st October. The gardens are open every day from 10.30 am to 5.30 pm and the house every day except Friday, from 11 am to 5.30 pm (Telephone: 01647 433306). Members of the National Trust are admitted free.

6. Stay on the Hunter's Path for a good ½ mile, ignoring a path on the left.

7. When the path forks bear right and follow the path down through the woods to a lane.

8. Turn right and the teashop is just ahead on the left.

Fingle Bridge was built about 400 years ago as a packhorse bridge across the Teign. Today the Teign valley at this point is a heavily wooded gorge but in living memory it was not so thickly wooded, as can be seen from old photographs, and people used to ride motorbikes up the steep sides. On top of the hills either side of the gorge are the remains of Iron Age hill forts, Prestonbury Castle to the north and Cranbrook Castle to the south.

9. From the teashop cross the lane and take the path directly opposite. This is the Fisherman's Path, by the river. At a weir, the path veers away from the river bank for a short distance. The informal path on the river bank soon rejoins it.

10. Stay on the path to the bridge crossed earlier in the walk. Do not cross it but continue on the right-hand bank of the river, soon leaving the wood.

11. At a road turn left, back to the start.

Walk 15
MANATON

This gentle walk is mainly through very attractive woodland. The quiet paths and tracks lead to the well-known beauty spot of Becka (or Becky) Falls so this is an ideal route for after a rainy spell when the falls will be in full spate. While not completely level, the climbs are very short and easy, making this an enjoyable route for all ages.

The Woodland Restaurant and Tearooms at Becka Falls are positioned within earshot of the cascade. There are plenty of tables outside, overlooking the river. Cream teas and a selection of cakes are served as well as full meals. The teashop is open between 10 am and 6 pm from Easter to November. Telephone: 01647 22259.

When the teashop is closed, an alternative source of refreshment is the Kestor Inn at Water, which serves bar meals.

DISTANCE: 3 miles.

MAP: OS Landranger 191 Okehampton and North Dartmoor.

HOW TO GET THERE: Manaton is a small village but it is very well signed from Bovey Tracey.

STARTING POINT: The car park near the church in Manaton (GR 749812).

ALTERNATIVE STARTING POINT: If you want to visit the teashop at the beginning or end of your walk, start at Becka Falls where there is ample parking in the car park provided (charge). Follow the signs to the falls and the teashop. You will then start the walk at point 6.

THE WALK

Manaton is in two parts, the old village clustered round the church and green and the newer part a little way down the road. Before the coming of the car Manaton was thought a good centre from which to explore Dartmoor. Two poetic visitors were Rupert Brooke who intended to return but was killed in the First World War, and Arthur Quiller Couch. The latter remembered Manaton in his lament for lost youth and love that ends 'For the want of her and Manaton, and the long while ago'. Manaton's most famous modern resident was also a literary figure. John Galsworthy lived at Wingstone Farm near Manaton for 18 years and during this time wrote his most famous books, The Forsyte Saga.

1. Leave the car park at the upper exit. There are two lanes, one either side of the village green. Turn left along the one on the far side of the green. After 170 yards, soon after passing the village hall on the left, turn right on an unsigned and unsurfaced track.

This path is known as Slinker's Lane. At one time the only pub in the village was the Half Moon, now closed but then in the long, low building overlooking the village green. Residents from the other end of the village used this path to slink up to the pub unseen.

2. After about ½ mile, at a T-junction, turn right on a public bridleway signed 'Water ½ mile'.

3. At a wide cross-path, where the path straight on is signed as private, turn right, signed 'Manaton direct'. This leads round behind buildings. At a T-junction turn right along a surfaced lane, passing some charming thatched cottages.

4. At a road junction turn left. Follow the lane past a farm and continue along it as it becomes a track. Ignore two paths on the left as the track bears right. Soon after this, the track narrows to a path.

73

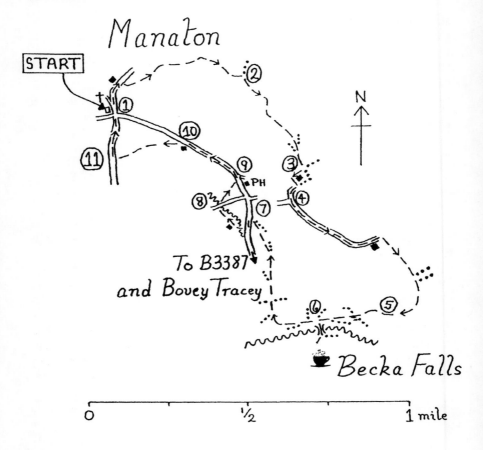

☕ **5.** Cross a stile into the woodlands which surround the falls. Continue on the main path, ignoring paths to the left and right, which are part of routes laid out by the National Park Authority. However, as you near the falls (you can tell by the sound!), divert left for a better view of them. The entrance to the teashop is over a wooden bridge on the left.

The falls plunge 70 feet over huge granite boulders and are an impressive sight when there is plenty of water. After dry weather the stream is rather concealed by the boulders and it is much less spectacular. The woodlands surrounding Becka Brook are a Site of Special Scientific Interest. The combination of soil, aspect and sheltered position has produced a very varied woodland with many ferns and lichens as well as flowering plants. The woods are perhaps at their most beautiful in spring when

74

many of the flowers are in bloom or maybe autumn when the changing leaves produce a blaze of colour. The woodlands are managed by the National Park Authority who have laid out various routes through the woods and maintain the paths.

6. After tea, return over the bridge to the path and turn left on a footpath signed 'Manaton', again ignoring all paths on the left and right. After crossing a stream and a stile, take the left fork to stay just inside the woodland.

7. At a lane turn left for 50 yards and then turn right over a stile. Follow the path across a stream, using the stepping stones, to eventually emerge on a lane.

8. Turn right. Immediately over a bridge turn left on a public footpath that leads to a road.

9. Turn left.
(For the Kestor Inn, turn right for 50 yards.)

10. After ¼ mile, immediately after the entrance to Mill House, turn left through a metal field gate. The path is not signed and is not apparent on the ground but it goes along the left-hand side of the first field. It continues across the next field to a stile to the left of a gate that gives onto a lane.

11. Turn right along the lane, back to the start.

Walk 16
HAYTOR

*H*aytor has long been a favourite with visitors to Dartmoor. Its distinctive crowning granite outcrops dominate the landscape for miles around and the summit is easily reached. This walk does not use the usual path, which can be very busy and is a rather boring route, though not difficult. The route chosen is even easier and, for most of the way, much quieter. From the summit of Haytor the views are unparalleled and after reaching the top, the walk is all on the level or downhill. It also visits the fascinating remains of the quarries and the famous granite tramway, once used to transport the rock. All in all, this is a walk full of interest and one not to be missed.

Moorlands Hotel has a lovely terrace and garden at the back where teas, including cream teas, toasted teacakes and cakes, are served every day throughout the year between 3 pm and 5.30 pm. Bar meals are also available. Telephone: 01364 661407.

DISTANCE: 2¹/₂ miles with an optional extension of 1¹/₂ miles.

MAP: OS Landranger 191 Okehampton and North Dartmoor.

HOW TO GET THERE: From Bovey Tracey take the B3387, signed 'Haytor', and continue to follow the signs. Park in the car park on the left just after the turning for Ilsington and Haytor Vale.

STARTING POINT: Haytor car park (GR 765772).

ALTERNATIVE STARTING POINT: If you want to visit the teashop at the beginning of your walk, park as described but turn right from the car park along the road for a couple of hundred yards to the Moorlands Hotel on the right. Return to the car park to start the walk as described.

THE WALK

1. Go to the far end of the car park. With your back to the car park look slightly right for the start of a path up the hill side. Make for this and follow it uphill to the top of the ridge, always bearing right at any junction.

2. At the top, turn right and walk along the ridge to a car park.

3. Cross the car park and the road and take the broad, obvious path up to the rocks on top of Haytor.

The views from the summit are truly outstanding, stretching away out to the coast and across Dartmoor. Today Dartmoor is seen as a precious and valuable landscape, guarded and protected by the National Park Authority. It was not always so: in the 16th century William Camden described it as 'Squalida Montana'. By the 19th century ideas had changed and the wild beauty of Dartmoor was attracting painters and writers among its many visitors. As it was so prominent, so accessible and had such stunning views Victorian tourists saw Haytor as the outstanding example of Dartmoor wilderness. To have climbed Haytor was to have 'done' Dartmoor and perhaps something of that opinion still prevails today. To help in climbing the rocks an iron staircase was built. This aroused the wrath of William Croker, a 19th-century Plymouth man who devoted his life to exploring and writing about the moor. He wrote of 'the unsightly stair step to enable the enervated and pinguedinous (sic) scions of humanity of this wonderful 19th century to gain its summit'. At least the plan at the turn of the century to build a coal powered electric tramway to the top was never realised!

4. After exploring the rocks, stand just to the right of the outcrop on the left, as you initially approached them. Look for a lower tor half-left. This is Holwell Tor. Make your way towards this. The path is not very clear to start with but soon becomes more obvious. Pass to the left of a disused quarry.

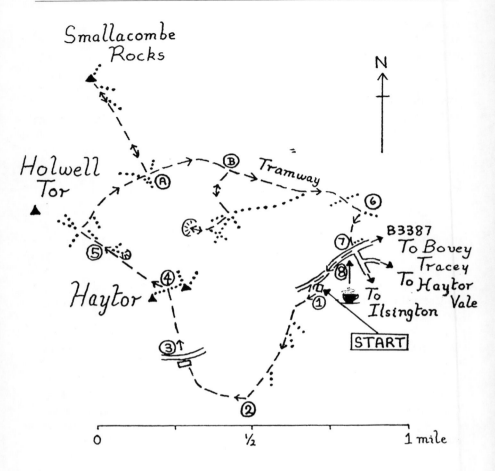

5. After passing the entrance to the quarry keep ahead through rock waste to the granite tramway. This can be recognised as two parallel lines of rock across the path. Turn right and follow the tramway.

The stone tramway was built in 1820 by George Templar to carry granite from the quarries on Haytor to the Stover canal at Ventiford; it was then taken to Teignmouth and loaded onto sea going ships. The project quickly became uneconomic because the rock had to be loaded and unloaded onto boats twice and use of the tramway had ceased by 1858. In the meantime the stone had been used for several important buildings including the British Museum, the National Gallery and London Bridge. The granite rails carried flat topped horsedrawn wagons and ran for over 8 miles, descending 1,300 feet. It was so well planned that, except for one short section, there are no cuttings or embankments.

To visit Smallacombe Rocks for further fine views (A):

Some 30 yards after a branch of the tramway joins on the left, take an almost level path on the left to Smallacombe Rocks. This diversion is strongly recommended to enjoy the breathtaking scenery. After drinking in the view, return to the tramway and continue along it.

To visit Haytor quarries (B):

Watch for a branch of the tramway on the right. Follow this to the quarry. Do not try to get into the quarry by the obvious entrance as this is soon fenced off. Instead, climb up to the left by a fence to a gate into the quarry. Retrace your steps to the tramway and continue along it.

The quarries are now a peaceful place to rest and linger. Nature has worked its magic on what was once an ugly industrial scar: the walls have become clothed in vegetation, producing a lovely natural rock garden, and the bottom of the quarry is flooded to make a little tarn with water lilies to complete the picture. The quarries are safe to visit, providing you don't try to climb the walls.

6. When you are level with a phone box, turn right on a wide path through the heather and gorse.

 7. Turn right along the road for 50 yards to Moorlands Hotel.

8. After tea continue along the road to the car park.

Walk 17
LUSTLEIGH

Much of this energetic walk is through superb woodlands and it gives an idea of what Dartmoor was like before ancient people cut down much of the forest cover. It is more demanding than many of the walks in this book as it climbs about 600 ft out of Lustleigh Cleave. However, apart from the woods and views, one benefit of all this expenditure of energy is that you will be able to tuck into a really good tea with a clear conscience. The return from Lustleigh is a short and easy stroll along very quiet lanes.

The Primrose Cottage Tea Rooms in Lustleigh are justifiably famous and are decorated to live up to their name. There is a lovely garden which overlooks Wrey Brook, and all the usual goodies, including cream teas and a mouth-watering selection of cakes, are served. Light lunches are available. Open every day between 1st April and 30th September from 10.30 am to 5.30 pm and until 6.30 pm on Sundays and bank holidays; also open at weekends in February and March. Telephone: 01647 277365.

When the teashop is closed, an alternative source of refreshment on this walk is the Cleave Hotel in Lustleigh, near the teashop. It is a charming 15th-century Heavitree house that serves afternoon teas and excellent puddings as well as a good range of pub food.

DISTANCE: 4 miles.

MAP: OS Landranger 191 Okehampton and North Dartmoor.

HOW TO GET THERE: Take the B3387 from Bovey Tracey towards Manaton and Widecombe. Bear right, following the signs for Manaton. At Reddaford Water turn right, signed 'Lustleigh 1½'. Just before the bridge turn left on a track to a parking area.

STARTING POINT: Drakeford Bridge parking area (GR 789801).

ALTERNATIVE STARTING POINT: f you want to visit the teashop at the beginning or end of your walk, start in Lustleigh. However, be warned that parking can be difficult. The teashop is in the centre of the village, opposite the church. You will then start the walk at point 11.

THE WALK

1. Walk back along the track to the road and turn left over the bridge. Take the first road on the left, signed 'Rudge and Sanduck'.

2. After 275 yards take a public footpath on the left, signed 'Hisley Bridge and the Cleave'. Stay on the main path by the river, soon entering woodland.

The Cleave is said to be haunted. Some report seeing a hunting party in Tudor clothes, while others say they have heard the sounds of horses and dogs, but when they turn round there is nothing to see ...

3. At a footbridge, stay on the same side of the river and take the wide rising track, not the path along the river bank. This soon reaches a T-junction with a cross-path. Turn left, signed 'Lustleigh'. When the track forks, bear right and this soon rejoins the other branch. At a second fork, a few yards further on, bear right.

4. After about ¼ mile, just before the track bends very sharply right, look for a path on the left leading to a stile over a wall. Take this path and follow it over the stile and uphill.

5. At a T-junction with a cross-path turn left, signed 'Manaton and Water' (not right, signed 'Lustleigh' - you don't get tea that easily on this walk!).

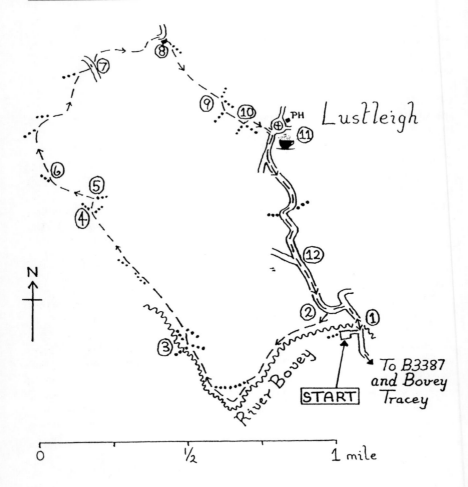

There are some superb views across the Cleave from this path.

6. When the path forks after ¼ mile, bear right uphill, passing two paths on the left. At the second keep ahead, signed 'Hammerslake', after which the path soon starts to descend and joins a larger path at a signpost and gate. Continue downhill through the gate to a lane.

7. Turn left for 30 yards and then take a signed path on the right and follow this downhill through the wood to emerge by a house.

8. Go ahead up the drive, past the house. Immediately after the house turn right on a path, signed 'Lustleigh'. Go through a small wooden gate and follow the path round to the right, not through the metal gate into a field. Follow this path to a cross-path by metal and wooden gates.

9. Turn right and follow the path along the right-hand side of the field to a gate. Immediately through the gate, take a path on the left, soon crossing a stream at a picturesque bridge of boulders.

10. Some 50 yards after crossing the stream turn left at a cross-path and follow this back across the stream and through the recreation ground towards Lustleigh church, seen ahead. Go through the gate at the end of the recreation ground and ahead, crossing the road, to the yellow building opposite the entrance to the church.

Lustleigh is a popular picture postcard village with rose-covered thatched cottages grouped round the village green and church. The church is on a very ancient site but was subject to heavy Victorian modernisation. A curate of the church, the Reverend William Davy, spent 50 years writing and publishing a System of Divinity in 26 volumes on a press he had built himself only to have it dismissed as 'a trifle', by the Bishop of Exeter. After the railway came to Lustleigh in 1866, the village became very popular with visitors, as it remains today, though now they come mainly by car. In the 1930s there were eleven trains a day. The railway has now been axed and the station is a private house. The stone bearing the often quoted epitaph to the station cat has been lost. It apparently read 'Beneath this slab and stretched out flat, lies Jumbo once our station cat'.

11. After tea return to the crossroads and turn left, signed 'Rudge ¹/₂'. Take the first lane on the left.

12. At a T-junction turn left then right at a road junction, back to the start.

Walk 18
BOVEY TRACEY

This delightful walk could easily take a whole day as there is so much to see and enjoy. It passes an important nature reserve and some fascinating industrial archaeology before going to the ancient town of Bovey Tracey for tea. The return route along the banks of the river Bovey is a real treat and there are many delightful spots in which to linger.

Brookside Tea Rooms, in a modern building on the edge of Bovey Tracey, directly on the route of this walk, are spacious and traditional. Outside there is a pleasant garden with several tables. A wide selection of tempting cakes is available as well as crumpets, teacakes and scones. For lunch, both light and full meals are served. Open from 9.30 am until 6 pm in summer and 10 am until 5 pm in winter. Telephone: 01626 832254.

DISTANCE: 6 miles.

MAP: OS Landranger 191 Okehampton and North Dartmoor.

HOW TO GET THERE: Take the B3387 from Bovey Tracey towards Manaton and Widecombe. Bear right, following the signs for Manaton. At Reddaford Water turn right, signed 'Lustleigh 1½'. Just before the bridge turn left on a track to a parking area.

STARTING POINT: Drakeford Bridge parking area (GR 789801).

ALTERNATIVE STARTING POINT: If you want to visit the teashop at the beginning or end of your walk, start in Bovey Tracey where there is a large public car park. Turn left from the car park and the teashop is on the right. You will then start the walk at point 8.

THE WALK

1. Go through a gate at the far end of the parking area. Continue along this track, ignoring all side turnings, until you reach another gate at a T-junction with cross-track.

2. Turn left and follow the track uphill to a road.

3. Turn left. After 25 yards take an unsigned path on the right to a gate into Yarner Wood Nature Reserve. Turn immediately left on a horse trail marked with blue arrows and follow it until it rejoins the road. Continue in the same direction along the road, passing the main entrance to the Nature Reserve.

4. At Reddaford Water pumping station turn right on a fenced track that soon narrows to a path. At a path junction continue ahead in the same direction, now on the Templar Way. Stay on the Templar Way when the path becomes a track again.

The Templar Way is based on the upper part of the line of the stone tramway built in 1820 by George Templar, hence its name. For more information about the granite tramway see walk 16.

5. At a road turn left. At a road junction by the Edgemoor Hotel turn right on Chapple Road. Ignore a public bridleway on the right at Whisselwell Farm. A small path on the right after a further 10 yards cuts through to join the line of the tramway and rejoins the road further on but is not a public right of way.

6. About 75 yards after the entrance to Chapple Farm, take a public footpath on the left along a farm track. At the farmhouse turn left and follow the track between farm buildings and on towards Bovey Tracey which can

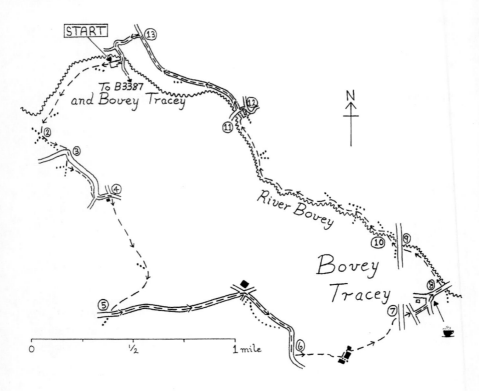

be seen ahead. At two gates take the one on the left, soon passing an old cross that once marked the grave of a Royalist officer and which has since been used as a gate post.

☕ **7.** Go across the bypass and take the public footpath almost opposite. At the road carry on in the same direction to a T-junction. Turn left and then right into Bovey Tracey at the next T-junction, where you will find the teashop.

There has been a town here since Saxon times. The name Bovey (pronounced 'Buvvy') comes from the river Bovey; Tracey was added after the Norman Conquest when land in the area was taken over by the de Tracey family from Traci near Bayeux. Sir William de Tracey was one of the party of knights who murdered St Thomas à Becket in Canterbury Cathedral in 1170. It is said that he built the fine parish church in remorse for his crime and the fact that it is dedicated to St Thomas à Becket may support the story. Today, it is a bustling town worth wandering around if you have time.

Bovey Tracey clay has been used in pottery for a long time. In fact, it was exported to Staffordshire by Josiah Wedgwood. Today there is a pottery of great interest to all those who enjoy their tea as it specialises in making teapots! It is on Newton Road towards the A38, not very conveniently placed for this walk but well worth a visit. It is open every day between 9.30 am and 5.30 pm and you can watch the teapots being made (Telephone: 01626 834441).

8. After tea continue in the same direction. Just before the bridge over the river take a path on the left into Mill Marsh Park and walk by the river.

9. Cross the bypass again and take the path directly opposite, turning right to continue along the river bank.

10. Immediately after crossing the river go down some steps on the left to continue along the river bank. Stay on the right bank of the river.

This stretch of the walk is always delightful but particularly in spring when the woods are carpeted with primroses, wood anemones, bluebells, violets and celandines.

11. Eventually the path bends right, away from the river. Ignore paths on the left which, contrary to appearances, do not have access to the road. Follow the path up onto the old railway track. Do not turn left along the railway but take the path on the left downhill to the road.

12. Turn left. After 50 yards turn right along a lane signed 'Lustleigh' to continue along the river bank. Soon the river bends away from the road. Sadly, there is no path along the river at this point so stay on the lane to a road junction.

13. Turn left, signed 'Manaton'. Ignore a road on the right and immediately after the bridge turn right along the track, back to the start.

Walk 19
EAST BUDLEIGH AND OTTERTON

This is a delightful and almost level stroll through attractive countryside between two charming Devon villages.

Otterton Mill has been grinding flour for the last 1,000 years and is one of the few surviving working watermills in England. Wholemeal and unbleached white flours are produced which are baked into the delicious bread and cakes sold both in the shop and the restaurant, the Duckery. This is open between 10.30 am and 5.30 pm every day in the summer and at weekends between the end of October and mid-March. There are plenty of tables outside in summer overlooking the river Otter. Tea and snacks are available on winter weekdays in the craft shop on the same site. Telephone: 01395 568521.

DISTANCE: 3 miles.
MAP: OS Landranger 192 Exeter and Sidmouth.

HOW TO GET THERE: From the A3052 Exeter to Lyme Regis road take the B3178 (this was the A370) at Newton Poppleford towards Budleigh Salterton. Turn right at the Rolle Arms into East Budleigh. The car park is signed on the left just before the church.

STARTING POINT: The car park behind the church in East Budleigh (GR 066848).

ALTERNATIVE STARTING POINT: If you want to visit the teashop at the beginning or end of your walk, start in Otterton where there are several spots where it is possible to park without causing inconvenience. The teashop is by the bridge over the river. You will then start the walk at point 5.

THE WALK

East Budleigh is a very attractive, unspoilt village with many cob and thatch cottages (see walk 10). It is mentioned in the Domesday Book as Budley and was a prosperous wool town in the Middle Ages. The church has over 60 carved pew ends depicting village life 400 years ago and these are worth taking time to enjoy. Among the motifs decorating the pews is the Raleigh family coat of arms and East Budleigh is best known for its association with Sir Walter Raleigh, born in 1552 at Hayes Barton, one mile from the village along Hayes Lane. The house, a modernised Tudor thatched and gabled farmhouse, is not open to the public. Sir Walter Raleigh was a statesman and author who enjoyed the patronage of Elizabeth I. He is mainly remembered today as an explorer of the Americas and it is commonly believed that Raleigh introduced tobacco and potatoes to Britain.

1. Leave the car park by the path to the church and go through the churchyard. Go straight ahead along Vicarage Road. After 150 yards turn left on a public footpath and follow this beside playing fields and along the right-hand side of a field to a lane.

2. Turn left for 200 yards. Turn right over a stile and walk along the right-hand side of a field. At the bottom of a dip, turn right on a clear path.

3. Immediately before the main road turn left on a lane to the church.

St Mary's serves the parish of Bicton, which is mainly the Bicton Estate. It is thought that there has been a church on this site since Saxon times. The rather romantic ruins in the churchyard are those of the Early English church in use until the 1840s. The present building was constructed between 1848 and 1850 by Lady Louisa Rolle in memory of her late husband. There is more information about the church available within.

Bicton Park can be glimpsed from the path just before you reach the church and

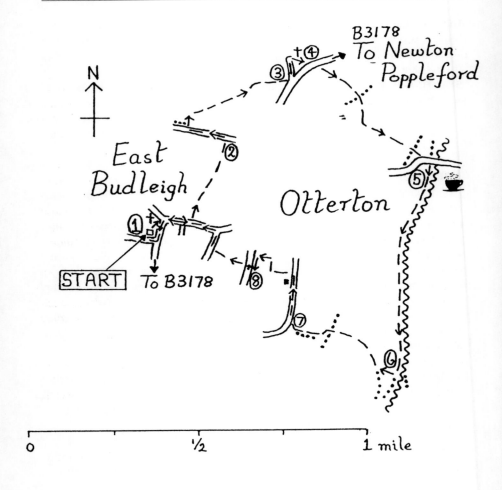

from the churchyard. These glorious gardens are maintained by a charitable trust and are deservedly popular. They are part of the grounds of Bicton House which is now an agricultural college. This enchanting place has a variety of different features which date from many periods. The Italian Garden, for example, was laid out in 1735, while the Oriental Garden was designed in the 1980s. The mild climate allows many unusual plants to be grown. The gardens are open every day from 10.30 am to 5 pm (Telephone: 01395 568465).

4. Take the path to the right of the church entrance to a road. Turn left for 40 yards and take a path on the right. (If you want to visit Bicton

Park, the entrance is about 200 yards further along the road.) Follow this clear path, going over two cross-paths, to a road. Turn left and continue over the bridge to the teashop.

There has been a village at Otterton for over 1,000 years. It is difficult to believe today but Otterton was once a thriving industrial centre with water powered woollen mills and a forge. At that time the river Otter was navigable but eventually it silted up and this strangled Otterton's further development.

5. After tea, recross the bridge and take the path on the left along the bank of the river Otter as far as a footbridge across the river. Do not cross this bridge.

6. Turn right and walk to a path on a raised bank. Turn right along this path, passing a small sewage plant and water pumping facility, to a track. Turn right to a lane.

7. Turn right. Some 75 yards after Rose Cottage turn left on a signed public footpath. After 20 yards take the path along the right-hand side of a hedge to a stile. Over the stile, turn right and walk round the edge of a field to a stile beside a gate onto a road.

8. Turn right for 20 yards and then take a public footpath on the left. At a lane turn right, then go left at a T-junction and left again at the church, down the High Street and finally right at Hayes Lane, back to the car park.

Walk 20
NEWTON POPPLEFORD

This walk starts at Aylesbeare Common, an airy, expansive place which is particularly attractive when the heather is in bloom in summer. It winds its way down off the common to Newton Poppleford for tea at its famous teashop and then returns by attractive and quiet paths to the start.

The teashop at the Southern Cross Guest House was run for 39 years by Miss McKenna and became famous far and wide for its amazing cream teas. Since her death it has been run by new owners who are firmly committed to carrying on its renowned traditions. The building dates back to at least 1748 but is probably older. It used to be haunted by the ghost of a girl and her dog. She was a recluse who never went out. In the 1960s some alterations to the house caused a staircase to be removed and the ghost went away, never to be seen again ... The tea room is open from 10.30 am to 6 pm and there are tables in the attractive garden as well as indoors. Telephone: 01395 568439.

DISTANCE: 4 miles.

MAP: OS Landranger 192 Exeter and Sidmouth.

HOW TO GET THERE: Aylesbeare Common is on the A3052 between Newton Poppleford and Exeter. Turn into the car park from a minor road, signed 'Hawkerland'.

MAP: OS Landranger 192 Exeter and Sidmouth.

STARTING POINT: Aylesbeare Common car park (GR 057897).

ALTERNATIVE STARTING POINT: If you want to visit the teashop at the beginning or end of your walk, start in Newton Poppleford where there are places to park without causing inconvenience. The teashop is near the junction of the A3052 and the B3178. You will then start the walk at point 6.

THE WALK

1. With your back to the main road look for a path about halfway along the left-hand side of the car park. Follow this for 50 yards and then bear right to join a track and turn right. When the main track bends left after 50 yards, take the wider of two paths on the right to a post festooned with blue and yellow arrows. Go straight across a track and continue in the same direction on a wide path for 1/4 mile.

If you examine the heather closely you will find that there are actually three different species present - true heather or ling, bell heather and cross leaved heath. They are supposed to like slightly different conditions, with cross leaved heath preferring wetter conditions than true heather and bell heather being found in the driest circumstances, but they often grow intermixed, as they do here. The ling has few leaves on the main shoots and the short side shoots bear four dense ranks of small leaves. The flowers are single and pale pinkish purple. The bell heather has leaves which can be tinged with bronze and curled over to protect the underside of the leaf. The leaves grow in a whorl or ring of three up the stem, each whorl giving rise to a leafy shoot. The flowers are a bit bigger than true heather, darker purple and are carried in a head or loose spike. The cross leaved heath has its leaves in whorls of four and looks quite grey because they are downy. The flowers are the largest of the three species, pink in colour and occur in a tight cluster at tips of the twigs. Gorse, which can have its bright yellow pea flowers at any time of year, grows among the heather. Remember the old saying 'kissing is in season when gorse is in bloom'.

2. At a post turn left on a public footpath marked by yellow arrows. There are many official and unofficial footpaths in this area. Ignore all unmarked paths and the first marked path on the right. After a further 225 yards the footpath marked by yellow arrows turns right off the larger path which

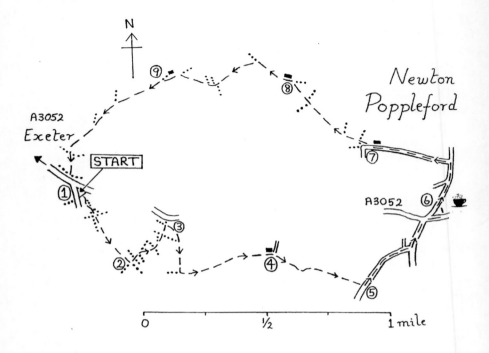

bears slightly left. Take the signed path and soon cross a track, continuing on the marked path.

3. Just before the road turn right away from it. Follow this path, first with a wood on the left, through the wood and then as its becomes a hedged path between fields.

4. At some cottages bear right uphill to eventually come to a lane.

☕ **5.** Turn left. At the main road turn left again and then turn right at the A3052. The teashop is on the left after 70 yards.

Newton Poppleford's name refers to its foundation as a new town in the 13th century by the Lord of the Manor of Aylesbeare, 3 miles away. Its church was built as a chapel of ease of Aylesbeare church in 1331 but it was completely pulled down and rebuilt in 1897. The toll house, which you pass on the right, was built in 1753 and is the oldest in Devon.

94

6. Leave the teashop car park by the rear entrance and turn right along the lane. Take the second road on the left.

7. At the top of the hill, 50 yards after a pair of houses, take a public footpath on the right by a seat. Continue ahead along a wide path, entering the RSPB reserve. As the path emerges from the wood onto the heath, ignore a path on the right and continue ahead to the drive of a house called Benchams.

8. Turn left. After 150 yards turn left on a public footpath indicated by purple arrows showing the East Devon Way. Stay on the main path, ignoring all paths to the left and right, to a drive to a house.

9. Turn left and follow the drive for about ½ mile, back to the start.